ON THE COUNT

A TRAVELER'S GUIDE TO PRISON

D1569393

ANONYMOUS

1

To My Daughter: I am so proud of you. I am sorry.

To My Queen: Thank you for always believing in me and for always loving me. A lifetime of love.

To My Mother: I am sorry I let you down but know that you raised me the right way. I just took the wrong fork in the road.

To My Father: I know you are watching over us.

Why The Name?

On The Count – The Traveler's Guide to Prison is best understood by those who have gone through the process of arrest, holding centers, jails, state prison and federal prison. It is similar in many respects to visiting a city, a small town, village or hamlet. Each has its own special and not-so-special identity. The same is true with the entire prison system. It is important to understand this because you need to know what to expect and how to conduct yourself within the different environments you encounter from arrest to freedom.

I still marvel at the inmates I have met who are new to prison life (I use the term prison interchangeably with jail, holding center and the like) or who have spent years and years behind bars (I use the term behind bars interchangeably with dorms and the like).

Some of the inmates who have been incarcerated for decades have never traveled, never seen the world let alone society beyond a few miles of their birthplace. All they have is prison. Whereas I may (and some of my readers) compare various hotels, cruise ships and restaurants, they will refer to different prisons as if they were hotels. It is interesting and often a sad commentary. I found myself doing this when I refer to the Tombs, Rikers Island, the Feds and the State facilities. Each has its own personality.

As this tome will demonstrate, I may alternate between comedy and tragedy because this is what prison life is all about. You will see the reason why I refer to prison as a microcosm of the world. Indeed there exists a society within each facility. Some are better than others. No different than the real (or outside) world. While very serious issues are discussed herein, I make it a point to impress upon the reader that how you handle your incarceration is solely up to you. Whether you laugh, cry, are a mean son of a bitch or treat everyone as they treat you, the time you are sentenced to serve will pass day by day. I chose to make the best of each and every day. Therefore, while each chapter will discuss important issues and describe the issues in detail, I have followed most chapters with an example or examples of related stories and events so as to allow the reader to have a image in their mind

of that which was discussed. Some of the topics may be humorous and other very serious. You'll see what I mean as you read on.

Forward

As my bio will demonstrate, I am an attorney by education.

This book does not intend to offer legal advice and if you are in need of legal assistance, seek a competent attorney versed in the field of criminal law. Do not even consider an attorney who does not specialize in criminal law.

The information contained herein is based solely on my experiences and is provided only as a tool to open your world to a world you may not be familiar with. My experiences in Federal, New York State and New York City may not be representative of the experiences of others nor how prisons and jails operate in other States and other local jurisdictions. Errors are my own.

To the dedicated members of the judiciary and their support staff, members of federal, state and local authorities, I commend you for your hard work and your efforts to protect society. You can sleep at night. To those who are members of the above who are dishonest, cruel or those who "use your hands" when you know you should not, I do not know how you sleep at night.

To those violent criminals who beat, rape and kill, karma is a bitch. To the remainder of the criminal world, our shared experiences would be a reminder never to forget our incarcerated experiences and to be productive members of society.

Let us make the world a better place. Let us also be aware of the old saying, "don't do the crime if you can't do the time." The system is corrupt, broken and needs to be fixed because many are doing too much time and some who have done the crime mask as if they are too good to do the time. We must really fix the system as it has gone wild.

I am complex. While politically I am a liberal with respect to domestic policies and the domestic agenda, I am conservative with respect to foreign policy and the foreign agenda.

On one hand, I am a quiet, generous person with the desire to help others. On the other hand, I can be a non-violent angry man, passionate yet polite, good guy and bad guy all rolled into one. Catholic schooling all my life, prayers daily, Church on Sunday. No desire to hurt others yet I have done so. I am very sorry and only actions will prove to those

Moving forward my sorrw.

I am not so much politically correct because I believe we have become a society where everything that happens turns out to offend someone. That said, I am very mindful of the feelings of others. While this book tells the truth and nothing but the truth with respect to my experiences, please understand that whether you are on the "good side" or the "bad side" I will tell it exactly as I have experienced it and with my opinions thrown in for good measure. It is what it is.

I have had the fortune and misfortune to experience varied aspects of the criminal justice system. Beside s being a practicing attorney, I worked in New York County Supreme Court, Served on a jury, spent time in Federal Prison, New York State Prison, County Jail and New York City Jail Including the infamous Rikers Island. I am confident I have sufficient expertise to provide you with interesting and informative information as well as entertaining you with true tales.

Blessed are you who are weeping, for you will laugh.
Luke 6:21

Beware the Fury of a Patient Man.
John Dryden

The Pen is Mightier than the Sword.
Edward Bulwer-Lytton

Why A Pseudonym?

The use of a pseudonym is to protect my family. If it were up to me I would proudly use my name and expose that which needs to be exposed. While I will consistently maintain my guilt, my shame, my embarrassment and my regret and remorse for that which I have done, the story needs to be told. It needs to be told so that naïve individuals, blue and white collar, black, white and every other color, race, religion and age young and old will stop and think many times over before they do bad and resort to criminal behavior. The impact on our families cannot be understated.

The criminal justice system, once its wheels begin turning towards punishing an individual, shows no mercy except perhaps if you have "influence." The lack of mercy extends beyond the individual and impacts that persons family and the public in ways that cannot be understood unless you are part of it. For that reason, it must be emphasized that the system is broken with flat tires for wheels because the system needs criminals. The prison system needs beds filled and regions such as Western New York need jobs. Again, this is not meant to imply that there should be no punishment but I do not want it to extend beyond me. Yes, my actions have had the requisite impact upon my family but the line in the sand is drawn when the impact by the criminal justice system crosses the line and holds someone for twice as long (and then some) as their own guidelines require. For that reason alone, the system is broken.

I mince no words and never will. If my name is disclosed I will name names. In the interim, I would hope that this book helps those who have made the awful decision to do wrong and have been caught. If you read this and have not been caught, stop what you are doing and just plain stop. Stop. Stop. If you have been caught, read this book carefully because the advice is raw and right. If you are a law abiding citizen, you too can get caught up in the nonsense. Do not think for a minute that it cannot happen to you.

For everyone else, you will understand why your taxes are so high when there are so many other alternatives to incarceration especially with the sheer amount of technological alternatives.

Hopefully you will understand that the story needs to be told but not at the expense of my family. I desire to avoid no one, deceive no one, nor do anything other than tell the story.

It is a story that must be told. I will tell it.

A Little Background

I was born and raised in Manhattan. While I had no silver spoon in my mouth, my hard-working parents struggled to pay for Catholic grammar school, Catholic High School and Undergraduate School and eventually Law School. In addition to working briefly for the Manhattan Supreme Court as a Law School Intern (I decided not to pursue Criminal Justice because I already sensed the corruption and injustice) I worked for a medium sized Law Firm. While there, I focused on Leveraged Buyouts. It was during the time of Ivan Boesky and the infamous "arbitrage" scandals. My exposure to the corruption of Wall Street became very real when I was assigned to work on a multimillion dollar credit facility for a multi million dollar store. While examining the documents, I asked a senior partner about the lack of a life-insurance policy in favor of the lender. Since the borrower received this private bank credit facility was up in age, I was concerned that the standard procedures were either neglected or ignored. The senior partner advised me to "shut the fuck up." I did so but made a contemporaneous note in my personal journal.

The loan closed and lo and behold a few months later I am reading the New York Times and an obituary for the borrower is a top story! Only a few hours later before the body could even get cold, I was summoned to the very same senior partner's office. In front of me were the senior partner, another senior partner and several bankers. All looked at me with burning eyes and the senior partner asked me about the lack of a life insurance policy. To make the long story short (many of my experiences are every long stories), I was saved by the contemporaneous journal I kept.

Thus, my feelings towards Wall Street nosedived.

I will not discuss much about Wall Street herein because that is another story. Its all about money, greed and the general public is clueless for the most part. Watching retirement funds loose money while bonuses are handed out. Why did the architects of 2008 not go to prison but the guy who takes a candy bar serves time? Why does Wall Street hate lower gas prices when the money saved by consumers will only serve to be put back into the economic engine. We have problems. I have a beautiful daughter who will be a practicing attorney very soon. My mom is great. My Queen the best. Yet I am stupid.

After I developed a distrust for the firm I worked at,

and realized they would eventually cease to exist because of their own issues (they eventually did), I left and formed my own practice.

While thriving and successful, and not for greed or a desire to have a private jet, yacht and jewelry, I fell into working for less than perfect clients. This caused my Federal and New York State prison sentences. Upon release, one gentlemen, a friend of the family offered me a position. This eventually led to doing some bad things for him. Not known to me were the other things going on. Upon his sudden passing, one son who is no angel himself, brought charges against me to essentially deflect the other issues. Once again prison. This time was really unreal Right after I pled guilty, I became ill with a spinal tumor which caused me to become wheelchair bound.

I had not only to deal with the prison time but in a wheelchair no less. The medical merry go round is further discussed herein.   In addition of of far more serious consequences was the impact on my family.

The loss of my father was an additional blow.

Fortunately we are strong, united and loving in a way many in this world are not. They have too been punished but the system and its built-in corruption and   desire   to   maintain   a   prison-business infrastructure is sickening.

There it is, my life in a nutshell. While it seems strange, it is all true. As stated, I am not using my name at this time. Hopefully, I need not disclose the skeletons in the closets of those who were involved especially one attorney and the son.

I have decided to put the past behind with no anger, and I can sleep at night. My family too.

I do not think some others can. They should not try to cast the first stone.

Guilty

The word deserves its own line. Interesting enough, you will find very few people in prison who are

13

guilty. In fact, most are innocent. That is, of course, if you believe them. I have heard the most outlandish explanations for the most heinous of crimes. They refuse to admit their own guilt. I will never understand how people can convince themselves that they are not guilty and expect others to believe them.

This book is different from most of the books you will read concerning prison life. I will delve into my background and how I landed behind bars. I will tell you the truth but I will also tell you the truth about prison. Most of what you read and most of what you see on TV does not tell the truth to the extent that if it did, no one would read or watch. A reader and viewer sees what the writer and director wants you to read and see in order to sell books and increase viewership. While prison is not a happy place (and I do not wish anyone to experience it), the public needs to know what really goes on. It is a business. While the belief is that its reduces crime and keeps the bad guys off the streets, many of the bad guys return to the street only to return to prison over and over again.

The revolving door exists. In the few years I was in State Prison, I have seen people go and return multiple times. One guy 5 times. Several 4 times. One guy was out only 18 hours.

There is no doubt that heinous people who commit heinous crimes should be locked up and the keys thrown away. What many do not understand is that the most heinous places that you see on TV and read about are for those heinous individuals. The rest of us wind up in facilities which, while not 5 star hotels, are quite comfortable. And they should be because many of us are not heinous. We may have done wrong and may need to be punished but we do not need to be raped, cut up, beaten and live a gulag existence. If you believe that we should be raped, cut up, beaten and live a gulag life, then you are wrong because one day, we will be walking down the street next to you, eat in a restaurant next to you (maybe even be your server or chef), work in the cubicle next to you and (heaven forbid) live next to you.

More shocking than the above is the fact that many who think they will never go to prison are also wrong. Perhaps it is that one extra drink. Perhaps someone makes an inappropriate comment about your wife, girlfriend or daughter. A fight ensues and before you know it, you are charged with assault. While many are "innocent" in prison, many are average everyday people who, but for a few seconds of bad timing, have to spend some time in prison telling their story about their innocence. I would venture to guess you even know someone.

I make no excuses for that which I have done but in reality, I am not such a bad person. Oh yes…in the sense that I did commit crimes, but I did not beat, cut, kill, rape. I did bad and deserve punishment. Most certainly so. I have been punished.

This book will explore in as much detail as possible the waste, the corruption and the abuse. Abuse of tax dollars and abuse of the system buy inmates and civil servants. You need to know the truth. You are paying for it. Those in the know do not want this information released because it may result in reform. Yes, not only do inmates need to be rehabilitated but the system needs rehabilitation also. I will explore some suggestions. Maybe someone will listen because rehabilitation is not taking place and if you wind up in prison, I do not believe you would want to experience what you see on TV. I believe you would want to experience what you will read herein.

I always wondered why on TV there was never a comedy about prison. Perhaps those in the know were afraid that if the truth were shown or a comedy

about the truth aired, people would write their representatives to turn all prisons into gulags. Or, maybe someone would want to commit a crime so they could enjoy prison. This does happen. Many commit crimes in the winter so they have nice warm place to live. I have had many inmates cry (and I do mean cry) pending their release because they had nothing to be released to. No family, nowhere to live, no love. Many deserve the loss of family and love and while I do not feel bad for them, chances are they may be right next to you planning a crime so they can go back "home." That is the truth and that is what the business does not want you to know about because the business does not rehabilitate. It only warehouses under the guise of punishment and instructions and treatment so that an individual can be a productive member of society. You will learn the truth about that too.

I debated whether to use real names in this book. I decided not to because I did not want to shame anyone nor shame their families and loved ones.

Many deserve to be shamed. Not because I have been shamed do I want others to also share the same fate. Rather, the truth comes out and if they are reading this book they know who they are and should share in embarrassment and remorse like me.

They know who they are. If you are reading this, you should be ashamed. Be it Prosecutors, Judges, Legal Aid attorneys, inmates, criminals, convicts, offenders, everyone who works as administrators, civil servants, many of you should be ashamed. Many of you also do a fine job and should be applauded and can sleep at night. As for the rest of you, I do not know how you can do it. I can only say that you too will have to answer to the Man upstairs.

Criminal Process

There is no attempt here to provide legal advice nor any attempt to discuss and/or describe the layout of a prison, a jail, a holding center and/or whatever else you want to imply herein.

It is important as you have heard in life to always make sure you have an attorney present at all discussions. I will not discuss pre-arrest, post arrest or any part of the legal process. What I will emphasize is the fact you will be transported a number of times to and from different facilities. Often and for the most part, these transfers will take place while in handcuff and perhaps other methods of restraint. It is best to be courteous at all times in order to avoid someone in authority "accidentally" make the restraints too tight. I have always been very courteous and I cannot tell you how many times they have been very generous in leaving the restraints off or very loose. I am not going anywhere and they know it. They also can and probably do relay to the next officer as to my conduct and this in turn makes the entire process easier. Believe me they talk about who is cooperative and who is the asshole.

More likely, each and every time you go to another facility even if temporarily, you will be asked

numerous pedigree questions such as name, date of birth, contact information and who to call in the event of an emergency. Likewise your family must keep a close watch over where you are and where you may be going. There may be times for security purposes that you and your family will not know where you are going but they can always contact the appropriate agency to track you if possible. Once you are in a facility for a certain fixed period of time, be certain to arrange a regular schedule of calls so that if your family does not hear from you they can contact the facility. Those in the know are well aware of who has people "outside" watching over their shoulder. Not only did my family have the telephone number of my facility but the local hospitals, police stations, state troopers and FBI. I cannot emphasize how important this is. Keep in mind that the authorities are duty bound to care and confine not to impose their own brand of justice or "hard labor."

While in processing, you may be put in a holding call with one or more and sometimes dozens of others. Maintain a quiet and respectful attitude without being too loud and don't tell anyone your life story. Maintain a dual line of respect which is important because you may meet these very individuals in your final facility. As a result, the respect and demeanor you displayed in the holding locale will not be forgotten. Remember not to discuss your case because you really have no idea who the person next to you is. Don't babble.

I have encountered people who have spread the word about me (all positive of course) when I got to Groveland. This breaks the ice. Remember that many of those you meet are in the system over and over again. I know people who get the same cell and cube and room as they return for violations or new bids.

While the word connotes such a lovely visual in your mind, reception is not really what one encounters. The purpose of reception is to classify you, provide you with some sense of orientation, provide physical exams and educational exams. Based on the results, you will be transported to a facility which will be your home away from home.

In New York, I believe that they assign the largest, expressionless Correctional Officers to the reception facilities. This is because there are some very dangerous people with you in reception. Some may have received a life sentence and have nothing to lose by killing, maiming or otherwise disrupting the person and process. The CO's for the most part have no idea of your background and perhaps your crime. Accordingly, they have to be prepared for anything as their safety as well as yours is of utmost importance.

I went into reception thinking the CO's were cast members from my favorite theme park and were there to present a story by taking the character of the storyline. In this case they play the straight face. Also, my fellow felons may also be part of the story line pretending to be possibly something they are not. So, it is possible the person next to you may in fact be a murderer sentenced to life or someone

facing only a few years for a DWI. Therefore many people put on the role of something out of the Gene Wilder and Richard Pryor characters in Stir Crazy. "That's right...we bad." Of course, sometimes they look stupid and at other times you are happy they are in fact in prison away from your loved ones.

I maintained a straight face, respectful, said as little as possible and just went through the process. You must shower (and believe me, many do need a shower), cut your fingernails and toenails (and believe me, many do need to do so), and get your hair cut bald. This I believe is not only to avoid lice and other fetid funk but also to bring your self-esteem down to as close to zero as possible. Some people really go nuts over this. Others do in fact have religious reasons for not cutting their hair and the department is generally receptive to this. If you have an appropriate religious reason for not cutting your hair, beard, or anything else, speak with your lawyer and then make the necessary arrangements so that you can keep your hair. These issues should be discussed at sentencing so that it can be Judicially Ordered. Make certain that you have a copy of the Order.

After the hygiene portion of reception, you then receive clothes. All of your street clothes go bye bye in the trash. Whether they wind up in someone's closet I cannot say but I do know they are supposed to discard everything. Take very little with you. You can bring your Bible, and some legal documents but it is better to have everything remain at home with loved ones who can then send it to you when you get to your assigned facility. It is better to follow this procedure because there are always guards who like to fuck with you and tell you to dump everything and refuse to mail anything home. Also, they will sometimes go through everything and read information about your case out loud and then start asking the other guards if it is ok to for you to take XYZ with you. Meanwhile, they are broadcasting your personal information in front of everyone. Also, some guards love to see you sweat and love to know that you are pissed off so just stay calm and go through the process without making their day.

That should just about conclude the first day except for medical. You will have an X-ray taken, a dental exam and then whatever appropriate inoculations required by law. If you refuse, it will not bode well for you. I always laugh at some poor ole' sole who is a drug addict and then gets defensive about receiving an injection. After years of taking drugs and shooting up, they suddenly concern themselves with proper hygiene. It's all bullshit but it seems they love to complain and it will only make the staff and guards get all pissy. Remember, you will have to go through the process anyway. The staff and guards will all go home at the end of their shift. Whether or not you are polite and go through the process or get angry and go nuts, they still go home...you do not get that privilege.

The first day will also acquaint you with state prison food in a prison setting. Really it is not that bad. In fact, better than many get to eat on the street. A lot of rice and pasta with few real potatoes except for fake mashed and some home fries here and there. There is a menu cycle of 8 weeks. Some foods repeat every week. oatmeal for example is every Monday. Other items like grilled cheese may appear every 4 weeks. The state has really cut back on providing a higher quality of food items. Breakfast Pizza, Scrambled Eggs, Fried Chicken Legs are all memories. Also, much of the food is laced with soy such as meatballs, hamburgers and meatloaf. If you are on a special diet for health or religious reasons, you may get better meals such as real ground beef hamburgers. However, nothing in prison comes without a price. If you are on a special diet, you are only allowed to skip 3 meals a week otherwise you will receive a Misbehavior Report, a $5 fine and have to pay for the food! Keep in mind however that if you are sincerely in need of a special diet, you may want to ask your attorney to also have this included in the Sentencing Order.

While in reception, the mess hall is a serious place. Again, no one knows who is next to them (CO's and inmates) so there is generally no talking and no fast movements. Take what you are given, go to your assigned seat which will be told to you by a guard and eat. Then get up when told to do so. In maximum security prisons in some facilities, inmates are not allowed to speak in the mess hall. When an inmate would finish his or her meal, the inmate would lightly "knock" on the table. This is a good thing to do because it lets those who are in the know observe that you know how things are done. It breeds respect. You never know who you may later meet in your bid who remembers you from reception. I have met inmates from prior facilities and believe it or not, people do remember. Better to have a good reputation than a bad one. Do not be stupid. A good reputation follows you and also makes your time easier.

You will meet with a nurse or doctor. Basically a triage system exists. They will determine what, if any medical care you need. Your blood tet results also determine what additional care you may need. Again, just like your legal documents, if you have any special medical needs, carry some proof of it with you. A guard may throw it away at intake but you can hope they will not. Also, have your family retain a copy of any medical needs, prescriptions, medical conditions which they can send to Albany if necessary. In other states or in the federal system, the same applies so please keep copies and records. remember, that you are in essence a "ward" of the state and they are responsible for your care, custody and rehabilitation. It is imperative that while you maintain respect for those who you encounter, if you act stupid, they will treat you accordingly. I have found that treating them with respect and courtesy goes a long way. Of course, there were occasions when it was necessary to have my lawyers get involved for certain matters, but only when it was absolutely necessary.

The health care professionals will also discuss your psychiatric status so again please be prepared. Do not say you are going to kill yourself if you do not mean it. They take such a statement very seriously and there are strict protocols which they will follow. I have met many inmates who are despondent and have had several show me prior cut marks and in fact, in Rikers, one inmate even sliced his wrists and then showed me his cut marks while bleeding. I hightailed it to a guard who promptly helped him and obtained emergency medical care. But he was treated and was right back in the dorm that evening. It went into his record and resulted in him going to a different facility than the one he would have originally gone to. I am sure he was going to a higher level facility. In New York State, there are several classifications for security, mental health and so on. You are regularly reviewed for either a higher level or lower level based on your crime, medical condition, mental health condition, etc. Your actions good and bad play a role in where you go and for how long. I would not attempt to act other than your normal demeanor because playing stupid will not work and may only serve to hurt you in the long run. As an aside, in your assigned facility, you do not want to play the crazy card because it will only result in the infamous "ten-day" trip to the Attica Mental Health Satellite Unit or such other similar facility. While I was fortunate not to have experienced such a trip, I am aware of and know several inmates who took the trip and regretted it.

If you take any prescription medications, take them with you and again, your family should advise the facility and provide copies. Sometimes, you may be given a generic version of the medication and/or an equivalent because the State Formulary does not provide for the medication you were prescribed by your personal primary care provider.

After all of the medical and mental health evaluations and examinations, you will be assigned a bed in a dorm or cell. You may have to share a "cube" in a dorm setting or a cell. Now you will start to interact with everyone. Remember the ground rules I have discussed. You should not believe your fellow felons, nor trust them. You do not know anything about them. Do not discuss your crime. I understand that my ground rules may seem difficult to handle but you are in a precarious situation and this is certainly not kindergarten.

Some inmates may have sex crimes or spousal abuse cases which are generally not very well received by other inmates. I remember in the federal system, my assigned prison in Allenwood, PA was not receptive to such crimes. When you arrived in the dorm, each inmate was confronted by several inmates to "show their papers." If you had one of those crimes, you were in for it. In the State system, in Groveland, the facility had a high percentage of inmate convicted of those crimes. As a result, there were few if any problems although problems did arise. Most of the inmates in Groveland who had those crimes admitted it and as such were treated pretty much the same as all the other inmates. The inmates who had problems were the ones who tried to lie about it and got caught in the lie.

Western New York

This chapter is a tough one. Western New York today is a lot different than Western New York years ago. Gone for the most part are the large industries such as Kodak, Xerox, United States Steel, Bausch & Lomb. These businesses were established decades ago by individuals who were born and raised in Western New York and as a result, their businesses, as they grew, maintained a very strong presence in the area. However, as time passed, these businesses, for various reasons, lost their cache and their importance.

Kodak for example, invented the digital camera but for reasons due to bad management, lost their share in the market and is only a mere shadow of its former self. Sad but true.

Tens of thousands of jobs have been lost forever. The weather is brutal for most of the year and as a result is a big drawback for any large business which may want to open back offices in Western New York. Many years ago, when I began practicing, I recall several large banks wanted to open back offices in Western New York. Rather than working with these potential large employers, the New York State government did nothing to attract them. They, instead, located down south with warmer weather and an eager and educated workforce. State and local governments were also more receptive and as such now have large banking centers in the warmer climates.

Recently, the Photonics industry has received hundreds of millions of dollars to locate portions of their infrastructure in Western New York but there is no guarantee that this innovative incubator of the future will actually produce the economic benefit many hope it will.

Western New York is thirsting for attention. There is tremendous animosity against the Downstate region. Statistics I have read in local newspapers show a lack of movement by the young towards higher education. There seems to be apathy towards going to college let alone graduate schools. Many who live in Western New York are in Western New York because there were born in the region, have families and therefore are "tied" to the area.

Enter the prison system. It is because of the above factors that prisons remain a prominent source of employment whether guards, civil servant "civilians," and medical personnel and other support staff. This is why whole families are employed in corrections related infrastructure including of course law enforcement. As an aside, it must be noted that there was a high profile prison escape in Northern New York which has a similar

economic tie to the prison system. It was learned that a major aid and abettor who worked at the facility was married to a man who also worked at the same facility. The system essentially feeds on itself and without the prisons, Western New York would be more of an economically sad region than it presently is. No matter what you say, this is the truth even though no one wants to admit it.

I remember the anger when Ralph Wilson, owner of the Buffalo Bills died. Whole newspaper pages were devoted to his passing and the concern that the Bills would move. Indeed, sports seems to give the citizens a psychological lifeline. The anger was evident when national news and New York City news reported his passing as a side story if at all. A repeat took place when the Bills were sold and the region felt reborn. A psychological lift! Unfortunately it was only scantily reported everywhere else.

A bright note are the radio morning shows which are better than anything New York City has to offer.

Funny, natural and real. Unpolished and truly fun. When two local hosts were fired in 2014 for on-air unfavorable remarks and comments, the uproar was unbelievable. I despised listening to the female co-host and many did but that made it more addictive to listen! Her husband, of course, works for Corrections as a guard it is believed. She and her male counterpart deserve national billing. I am glad they returned to the airwaves in the afternoon on another station which also has a delightful morning show. I stream them today and hats off to them and all the morning shows. They kept me laughing at times when I was down. I am sure they do likewise for many listeners and wish them well.

The State of New York can, if they really wanted to, make relocating for big industries a possible happening if our esteemed elected officials (at least those not indicted for alleged criminal behavior while in office and several who were convicted) would lower taxes. It can be done but unfortunately political corruption ruins the State and its citizens suffer for it. When the governor closed prisons in the region, the vitriol was unbelievable. Prisons should not be the only source of life in the region. this is no joke. It is like Siberia and there is no excuse for the State Government to rely solely on the prison industry which then creates the need to keep the beds full.

If you do not believe me, read the February 27, 2015 editorial in the Wall Street Journal, "Andrew Cuomo's East Berlin" where the region is described as desolate and an economic bummer.

I included this chapter because if you are assigned to a facility in the region, you will encounter your prison to be a small town where all the employees know each other and may in fact and often are related to each other. This breeds problems for if you have an issue with one employee, you will quickly learn that you now have a problem with many more employees. It is not uncommon for some of the inmates to know and/or be related to some of the employees.

Housing

Depending on the facility, location and classification, your home away from home will vary. This is why your conduct during reception will play a role in the final determination of where you will spend your time. I have been to various federal, state and local facilities and their type is as various as a Budget Inn as compared to a Ritz Carlton and from a regular room to a suite. You must be ready to accept this. there is no choice.

A cell is a cell is a cell. Steel bunk with a 1 to 3 inch mattress. Steel toilet bowl and sink combination. That is it. A light overhead which may or may not be controlled by you. Your door is either steel with a slot for you to put in your hands or to receive food. You put your hands in to be cuffed if you are moved around the facility for any reason if it is deemed that is the procedure in the particular facility and/or because of your conduct. In Rikers, if you are violent and/or prone to use weapons, you will wear a special "mitten." If you are prone to spitting, you may wear a clear plastic face plate. Remember that your conduct plays a role in how you do your time but you are going to do your time regardless.

Laundry may or may not be done in the particular facility laundry in which case you are provided with

a net bag. Your laundry is washed and dried while in that bag which you knot on top. Often, your laundry comes back wet. In some facilities, you may be able to arrange a "contract" with another inmate who for a price (maybe a pouch a month) will wash and dry and fold your clothes. If you can afford it, this method is recommended. If the facility does not do laundry, then perhaps that steel sink or the shower is the laundry facility for you!

Soap and toothpaste and toothbrushes are provided and also toilet paper. It is suggested that you ration your toilet paper as each facility will distribute toilet paper according to their own schedule. In Rikers, we were not provided with a roll. Instead, we were provided with "x" amount of sheets which needed to be requested each and every time we needed to use the facilities. In some prisons, you can purchase your own toilet paper in the Commissary.

Your facility may or may not have air conditioning. More often than not, the temperature is not what you desire. In some prisons, you can purchase portable fans which clip-on to your bed frame.

Most of the time, cells and dorms are in sections known as blocks within sections known as houses

or vice versa. It is common for you to be asked "where do you lock" when asked for your location. Many State forms, when a line is provided for you to insert your location will ask for "cell" which I cross out and would insert "dorm." No special reason except for the psychological benefits!

A dorm is much better in my opinion but I have met many inmates who rather have a cell. Sometimes I think they are just bullshitting and trying to portray toughness. Keep in mind you are living with a bunch of guys sometimes up to one hundred in a small area with your own room or cube. Just enough for a bed, locker and small locker. Always keep your personal belongings locked and away from prying eyes because your fellow inmates will be able to see everything and anything. It is called "clocking" and the less clocked you are, the better for you. Don't worry but as I have repeatedly said, take it slow in the beginning and you will not have a problem. Just do not show off.

The federal facility in Allenwood was air conditioned with pleasant dorm style furniture in your cube. All was spotless and fine.

Rikers is the Budget Inn compared to the federal Ritz Carlton. I would place the "Groveland Resort and Spa" to a mid priced Marriott with no air conditioning but comfortable in all other aspects. The State is phasing out the 3 inch mattress with new 5 inches (approximately) which are comfortable. Believe me, you can survive. My family ordered linens from a company which provides mail order service to inmates. I received bed sheets, towels and dry goods so that I did not need to use state supplied linens. This is not possible in the federal system as they do not permit packages.

A potential problems is when you are "double bunked" or "double celled" because who gets the top bunk is dependent on how tough the other guy is and how the chips fall. Also, keep in mind you are now sharing space with a stranger who may or may not bathe in an area the size of a small walk-in closet. Again, you have to use your judgment and see who he is aligned with before you complain. What this means is that if your "celly" or "bunky" is a gang member, you may want to think twice about complaining.

Some individuals may have a bottom bunk based on medical needs or age or weight. Yes, I have seen 400 pounders in a bottom bunk sharing with a 120 pounder on the top bunk. Again use your judgment and be aware of your surroundings.

Most Dorm officers maintain a list of pecking order

so that you will be moved from a top bunk to a bottom bunk to a single cube or cell in a fair and proper order but of course there will be some kiss asses who will get what cue they want faster than others. You will quickly learn by observing who these special guests are in no time.

I do not like "rats" and you will find some not only the animal kind but the human kind. I have been known to give the human rats cheese and pen and paper to help with their ratting! The animal kind is hard to find (fortunately) in the federal and state systems but you may find (and be prepared) to find them in your local facility. It is not a pleasant site. I will go so far as to say I have never seen a rat other than the human kind in the federal and state systems. The respective governments do not want a health catastrophe lest massive class action lawsuits and do a very good job in keeping the facilities as clean as possible.

Dorm Life

Remember simple rules. Keep quiet about what you see going on, mind your own business and don't gamble and do not owe anyone.   In another chapter we will discuss and explain con games but use common sense not to open doors. If they see you giving out coffee, you will become the local Starbucks and everyone will be asking you for coffee, sugar, creamer, cigarettes, lighters, etc. You will become the local bodega and the news will travel fast across the compound. Do not fall for this ruse nor allow yourself to gain a reputation as an easy mark.

Keep your cube clean. As with anything, you can pay to have someone clean it, cook for you and do your laundry. In the federal system, you can pay with a commissary buy of a few dollars every week, every two weeks or every month or however you negotiate a fair arrangement. The same holds true in the NYC system. In the state system, you can do the same or pay with stamps or "pouches" of tobacco every commissary buy. Laundry service was one pouch (approx $3.19) every month. Cleaning service which included dishes averaged one pouch every commissary buy which is every two weeks. I had a friend make me fresh coffee every morning which also provided him with a cup. Fresh coffee in the morning in prison makes a big difference to getting your day off on the right foot!

Some inmates do not shower. I will never understand why but I enjoyed the "spa" experience every day and sometimes twice or three times depending on weather, exercise, etc. I bought some "Muslim oils" which is basically brand name designer cologne sold for $1 as a donation to the Muslim population. They are sold in little vials similar to what you are given in a department store.

You can add the oil to a spray bottle and "mist" the spa when you shower. I called it the true spa experience and it made shower time more enjoyable. After some time, many were calling the shower the spa!

I rarely watch TV at home so I bought a nice radio and listened to all my radio shows which I do in bed at home, my car, and whilst traveling. It keeps me up to date and educated unlike many of those you will reside with. Also, the TV and the TV room causes the biggest fights so I was not comfortable being in that room.

Never ever gamble no matter what your friends say as you will have trouble either owing or trying to collect. Do not get caught up in the small little card game which foments fights.

Some inmates establish a "store." Basically they will sell popular items which some inmates either cannot buy at the commissary because of some restriction or because they are in "dire" need for a soda, popcorn or a honey bun. of course, the purchase comes at a price. For example, a honey bun which costs about 45 cents will cost 2 honey buns in return. This populates the store owners inventory. Sometimes you can get 2 honey buns for 3 in return. The store keeps the store owner in the black while providing a useful service. It is not permitted but most guards tend to look the other way.

Meals

In some prisons, you must go to the mess hall once, twice or even three times a day. If you have the option, and can avoid it, do not go. This is where the CO's really get their jolly's searching you on the way in and out for that extra piece of bread or an orange (no kidding) or just harass you while eating. It is akin to being the animal in the zoo and the co's are the visitors. I never gave them the satisfaction and opportunity because if I went to the mess hall I never took anything out with me and for the most part did not go at all. For the record, I referred to the mess hall as the restaurant.

I bought oatmeal, cereal and bread, pop-tarts for breakfast and always had enough food to make my own meals, cook with others or even just a peanut butter and jelly sandwich. Sometimes I ate very light for the day, I fasted other days. You can do it otherwise you will be eating soy laden with starches three times a day every day and look like an elephant from the very zoo I have mentioned.

I also do not snack at home but did keep some popcorn and some treats which I enjoyed once or twice a week often on weekends as a treat and something to look forward to. It makes the time go fast. It is amazing how many will cook at 10pm a full meal and then go to sleep. Not healthy and you do not need to get sick in prison.

Drink plenty of fluids. I always drank a lot of water at home and did likewise in prison with only one cup of coffee. I enjoy a diet soda at home and would once every other week enjoy a diet soda. In summary, keep a well balanced diet. You can do it. By the way, always keep a can of ginger ale and some antacids in case I got sick but never did.

As discussed prior, there are special diets but if you are on a special diet, you are required to go to the mess hall.

You must always be aware of your surroundings. If there is a fight in the mess hall and you get caught up in it either being part of the altercation or just in the wrong place at the wrong time and it is believed that you may have been a participant, you could get a serious misbehavior report. Such a ticket can put you in the box and be charged with inciting or attempting to incite a riot. As unbelievable as that may seem to you, it is not out of the realm of possibility. You must always remember that you are no longer in your world. You are in their world and their world is a lot different from your world. Thereis a lot of thinking and doing which may seem dysfunctional and which sometimes is but that is the way it is and will be while you are in prison.

Correctional Officers

It is common in any business, military and profession that these is a disparity among various levels of authority and the competency of such individuals. The same holds true within the correctional system. While I may have done bad as a lawyer, I was never incompetent so we must analyze individuals based on the individual.

The federal system is interesting because the officers interact rarely with the inmates. They do not engage in conversation nor harass nor bother inmates unless, of course, the inmate does something calling for such action. I spoke with no CO's during my federal time except for those who I spoke with as part of my job as a mess hall clerk. During those hours, they were polite and professional and would let their hair down so to speak. They wore blue uniforms with blue sports jackets and a clip on tie lest they run the risk of being chocked during an incident. The authority of the federal government was apparent and I cannot say enough for their professionalism and respect.

The state system is a lot different. For some reason the guards are as different as night and day. There is much more interaction with a lot of name calling and horseplay. Some guards do so in a very positive way almost like kids at play while others are just nasty and downright a disgrace to the profession. They must realize that the majority of the inmates will be released. Also, many of them know the inmates from their hometown and vice versa. In Rikers Island and the NYC system, the same "fun" takes place but in a positive way. It is hard to describe the NYS guards except to say that you learn fast who are the good ones and who are the bad ones. Of course, the NYC system does have it share of bad apples including some officers who have been charged for allegedly committing very serious offenses.

One in particular in New York State was, so bad, it was necessary for me to tell my wife who then called the Albany Inspector General and one of his investigators visited me with a file several inches thick documenting in detail his alleged drinking and even driving into the front gate of he facility causing over $100,000 in damages. I kid you not as this matter was too serious to inflate.

It is important to state that the majority of the Correctional Officers I have met are hardworking family men devoted to their families and also to their job. Interesting enough, one of the officers told me that when he is actually performing his duties according to the book, he gets ribbing and sometimes serious feedback for the higher ups and his fellow officers that he is being "too nice." That is not their job. They are essentially guards to make sure we don't hurt each other or them and hat we serve our sentence. They are not supposed to "punish" unless of course we deserve it by some overt action on our part.

The system is rife with nepotism. It seems that everyone is related. Since the facilities are for the most part located in small towns, there seems to be a common mind-set that when someone male or female in the family is of age which for the state system is twenty-one years old, they will become a guard. Albany, I am positive, must be aware of this but has no policy against this form of hiring and looks the other way and allows it.

Many positions in a facility have one guard assigned even though there may be several guards working that job. These are called "bids." Just as an inmate is doing his or her bid, so too will a guard. In fact, they even tell you how many years they have served and how many years they have left till they retire. A major difference of course is that they get to go home at night. There are statistics which I could not confirm that guards suffer a high rate of divorce, suicide and health issues. I know of several who had heart attacks, died and a few who died right after they retired. I must say that unfortunately, the ones who were really upstanding were the ones who died. I pray for them and their families.

I also could not confirm, but no one has denied, that there is some kind of consideration passed in order to get the bid a guard wants. Some of the bids are, for example, being the head guard in a dorm, or the front gate or a guard hut in the yard. The assignments vary and can be easy or difficult. Some guards want to sit in a chair and sleep all day or night, while others want to work in maintenance or the mess hall where they are on their feet and being productive. This is all subjective. Some are "plum" assignments according to the guards while others are "torture." Many guards, after they are in the system for awhile, enjoy "trips." These can be medical, court or funeral trips which may be all day, or a few days with overnights. The overtime makes these bids worthwhile and lucrative in addition to carrying a weapon.

Although I call them guards, I always addressed the guards in their official capacity. I always addressed them and the civilians and everyone else in the system as sir, madam, miss, officer and the like.

Even the officers I would sometimes chat with about politics were addressed by me in their official capacity. It is important to understand that I would never speak to an officer about anything beyond a few words of greeting unless they spoke additionally with me. Even then it was very surface and short and sweet.

This is important because under no circumstances do you want to be branded as a friend of the cops just as a cop does not want to be branded as a friend of the inmates. Very important. There were some situations where a sergeant wanted to speak with me. It was always to fish around and try to ascertain if there were any issues going on in the dorm. Anytime I was called to their office I always brought another inmate as a witness.

Credit Deserved

I know I have made a decision not to name names. I have already stated and explained that I do not want to create controversy or chaos by naming names. Notwithstanding the above protocol, I am confident that many readers will know who the individuals are that I am discussing in this book.

There are many more worthy state civil servants than unworthy. The financial waste to the taxpayers with money being spent on new vehicles, lawnmowers, windows, flooring is sad and all you have to do is visit a prison to see guards lying around with some sleeping, workers doing nothing but drinking coffee or even taking the day off. The welding program was shut for weeks because the civil servant instructor was absent. I have heard rumors that he had a side business (as many do) which required his presence. In fact, because of the special arrangements the Union must have negotiated, many of the civil servants and especially the guards can work double shifts for several weeks or months and then take months off at a time. I am confident that this type of special coddled arrangement does not exist in the private sector and I cannot believe that the taxpayers are not somehow getting screwed.

There are many wonderful officers who deserve credit for their professionalism. Sergeants who also were worthy of praise as well as a few lieutenants and higher ups. One sergeant was a foster parent for (I believe) 8 foster children. This particular official who has since retired deserves blessings not only for his real world contribution to society but also for the respectful manner in which he treated the inmates and staff. Generally, I learned that if a civil servant treated us like shit, he did so as well with his or her fellow civil servants. Once again, the inmate you mistreat may one day be your neighbor.

Another sergeant would have inmates sing songs and holiday caroling if their door or locker was not locked. He could be tough when necessary but he knew how to maintain order while still conducting himself in a professional manner. This particular sergeant has since retired and once again, I wish him only good health and an enjoyable retirement well deserved.

Then we had the sergeant who openly told everyone in the wheelchair section that he would beat the shit out of anyone who caused a problem. This was his greeting the first day he was assigned to the wheelchair dorm. In fact, he was the one who caused the problems. I wonder if it is possible he could beat the shit out of himself. His wife was a nurse in the infirmary. She was the polar opposite of this sergeant. She would bake for her colleagues various breakfast treats and always smiled. She conducted herself professionally and never ever mistreated any of the inmates. Perhaps love truly is blind. As a postscript, this sergeant became a lieutenant and retired very soon thereafter. Another example of the complexities of the civil service system. If it is possible for an individual to obtain this special treatment and benefit, then I guess that individual should receive these benefits but certainly something fishy is going on with the manner in which the system permits these maneuvers at the taxpayer expense.

Hopefully, Only One Of A Kind

I had difficulty pondering over a title for this chapter. I do not want to exaggerate the seriousness of certain events which I witnessed nor disparage above and beyond the individual who was number one in my book (and I am confident many others whether guards or inmates) for being a disgrace to his profession and his fellow guards. I arrived at Groveland in November 2010 and immediately I was told about guard S who was on leave or vacation and would not return until January or February of 2011. Of course, there was no way anyone could properly describe him. He had the 11pm to 7am shift or tour in guard parlance. Normally, I was asleep during those hours or at least until 5am. I figured I would sleep through his shift and thus avoid any problems (fortunately I did for my entire stay). This particular officer/guard left on all the lights by his "bubble" which is the area where the guards sit and have their file cabinets, storage, a bathroom, etc. Basically a little office which may or may not be enclosed by Plexiglas hence the name "bubble." Generally, the overnight guards will shut all the lights. There are some night lights which may or may not be left on in the facility. In our case, the night lights were quite bright and some of the guards would shut them off as the chance of trouble was minimal. However, some of the sergeants or higher-ups required them on. I must add that there are instances where the guards would leave the lights on if an individual was ill or if there were medical emergencies. In our facility, we did have ill inmates and sometimes did have medical emergencies during the night. With that in mind, there really was no valid, practical need to have all the night lights on and the lights in the bubble and the lights surrounding the bubble on. Rumors were always swirling that this particular guard was afraid of being the target of some angry inmate but I had no way to determine the veracity of those rumors. This particular guard, when I did encounter him while going to the restroom or after his shift, was always polite and cordial. With me that is. During his shift, he would read the newspapers and then tear them into small pieces and put them in the trashcan which he would remove from the bathroom. There may have been a penological need for this but I am not aware of any such need. He would then yell in the loudest of voices: "Count Time." Of course everyone would wake up. I could understand the need to yell before the 6:15am count but this also was for the 11pm count. Explanations of the count process will be discussed further in this book. The last count of the day was generally around 10:15pm. The guard would then leave around 10:40pm and the new guard would come in around 11pm. This count and all the counts during the night were done by the guard walking around and checking to make sure everyone was tucked in. I concluded that he either wanted to make sure everyone was alive or that he did this to be a prick. Since no one else followed this method of counting, I am forced to conclude he was just being a prick.

When I first was assigned to the particular dorm in question, my cube was positioned so that I could see the bubble. Many nights this guard would actually spit or blow his nose onto the wooden railing that everyone including inmates and guards as well as civilians would touch. Additionally, he would take coats, laundry and anything he could see left around and toss them in the garbage and then add disinfectant.

I could write a book based solely on this guard but there are a few situations which I am compelled to discuss. One day, I was scheduled for an outside trip for medical purposes. It was early am and the routine was to bring me to the medical center where I would be inspected, shackled and then brought to a wheelchair van for my trip. On that day, I was waiting in the lobby of the infirmary and there were several guards around because it was shift change. The guards were laughing and talking which was not uncommon but then I realized they were talking about this particular guard in question. It became apparent that, while allegedly intoxicated, he drove/banged his car into one of the little green painted school buses used to drive around the compound. That vehicle then went into the front gate of the complex causing (I later learned) over $100,000 in damage!

Once again, I could not make this story up if I wanted to.

Uncle Sam

He did look like Uncle Sam and was delighted to yell and scream at the top of his lungs when you went through the metal detector in the activities building. I used to enjoy watching his face turn beet red for the most stupid of reasons. I never gave him an opportunity to ever speak to me and I would remove my glasses when I entered the building as if not to "see" him nor acknowledge his existence.

One day it was snowing heavily and you could not enter the building until 15 minutes before an activity (in my case religious services). He told me to wait outside. No yelling just a firm "command" to wait outside. I went outside and waited in the snow. I did not care if I froze to death as I would not allow him the pleasure to say no if I were to ask (beg) permission to wait indoors. Well, after a few minutes he told me to come inside. reverse psychology with some of the creeps that derived a sadistic pleasure worked with them.

Not all civil servants were bad. I felt sorry for a guard who retired and dropped dead a few days after. He was never able to enjoy the retirement that he worked so hard for decades. The State reaped a benefit for his service and he never had a chance to enjoy what he deserved. Never will I understand why the good ones die and the shitheads live.

Ugh's

Three Correctional Officers fall into a unique category because together they share one brain. Officer C is, of course in my opinion, a bipolar ADHD who wears ill fitting trousers. He is constantly twitching, standing on one leg and then the other, cursing one minute and calling everyone "young man" the next. A perfect example of his intelligence or lack thereof was when one day, I was in the infirmary waiting to pick up medication. The procedure called for an inmate to leave his ID card on the front desk and wait to be called. A simple enough procedure. Not enough for CO C to handle without creating confusion and calamity. He was sitting and then standing and then sitting and then twitching as inmates came in the front door. One inmate asked him where to place his ID card and then he started yelling and cursing at the top of his lungs (in front of several female nurses who just looked down and shrugged) and berated the inmate for being a "filthy, smelly, infected fucking piece of shit." He stated that, "who the fuck do you think would touch your ID card, certainly not me you filthy fuck." Then...he picked up all the ID cards with his hands anyway! No promotion or rocket scientist position for this "young man."

Officer M is another genius. He is about 6'4" and 20 pounds when wet with a constant mouth and lip twitch and a penchant for constantly playing scratch-off lottery tickets. Another foul mouth in front of women. He loves to work the mess hall with his "twin brother" who is 6' and 250 pounds.

Only in Western New York can twins like this exist. Both of them, when working in the mess hall will search you only to find nothing. There is nothing to steal. Maybe a slice of bread or an apple. The funny part is if they find something, they make you throw it out in the garbage. Rumor has it that one of them has an agreement with a compost to bring the garbage over.

Another officer we shall call M is also obese and also a filthy mouth. Working the mess hall as well he has 4 children with 4 different women (at last count). The only positive is that he is a war veteran and I do appreciate his service. He is a smart as one rock. Anyway, same as above with respect to his conduct except he yells at you for stealing state food while he is eating state ice cream. Another rumor which I cannot substantiate but has some possibilities is that the line for the mess hall is always long on hot dog days and that this is because the CO's call many of the houses at the same time to discourage you from going to the mess hall and as a result they can keep the leftovers! The rumor has merit because BBQ grills were always on during hot dog days.

This gives you a sampling of what is in store for you. Stupid, dumb but dangerous so just observe, listen and obey orders. Remain observant at all times and enjoy the freak show.

Fellow Inmates

Prison is a microcosm of the world we live in. The only difference is that in the world or the "street" as it is called, we do not interact on a daily basis with this cauldron of people. For that reason, tension rises and problems occur.

It is interesting that I have met many individuals both inmates and civil servants alike who are no different than people we meet in the street. But for being in prison, we may have never met as our worlds would have never mixed.

I have been fortunate to meet very nice people even though they are in prison for a variety of charges. Keep in mind that to judge is to be judged and there is no excuse for looking down on someone in prison. The opposite is true, if you give respect, you will receive respect. Inmates do look up to older people, educated people and those who show respect. Many times, inmates may have been born poor, in a family where the father figure is absent and perhaps in jail also or dead. The life experiences are slim to none including lack of proper education which some never learn to acknowledge has been the true cause for their prison life. I have no excuse in this area because I grew up with both mother and father. No siblings but an extended family. Education thru the roof. No excuse but because my family was middle class and I grew up on the Lower East Side of Manhattan, I was able to understand the "other" world. For that reason, I have had tremendous respect afforded to me and have been fortunate to have no problems in prison.

I have actually had inmates come to me and tell me that if anyone bothered me, they would take care of it. Believe me they would because some have nothing to lose as prison is their home especially some who have been incarcerated for decades with no chance of getting out.

Even those inmates have a soft side. Keep in mind that the real bad guys as we say are locked up in Max's (Maximum Security Facilities which can be called Penitentiary, Max A, Max B, Supermax, etc. That is another story but for the most part, the inmates I met will provide a tremendous amount of respect and can be enjoyable company.

Having studied psychology, I tried to do some diagnostics including myself. I have OCD...Obsessive Compulsive Disorder. Not the kind where I wash my hands hundreds of times per day but a kind of OCD which makes me very neat and organized. It helped me in my practice and hurt me also. That said, I have met a huge number of inmates who would probably be in some type of state government run mental health facility were it not for the fact that few exist. Prison is now the new psychiatric center of state run facilities. Problem is it is broken and does not work. I have had close friends (inmates will use the popular word acquaintances, who had serious disorders and had to wait weeks and months for treatment. Even though

they wrote to the Office of Mental Health it does not work. It is sad and it is wrong because money is wasted and little treatment exist.

If an inmate goes too far begging for health, they are considered a danger and then go on a "10 day trip" to Attica where they are evaluated. What is the end result of this evaluation period: absolutely nothing. A few days before writing this chapter, an inmate who had previously requested OMH had a breakdown in the Peterson Building. What happened...a Sergeant stomped on him with his boot to the inmates head. Beat the shit out of him with a few other CO's. The inmate will never be seen again. Wrong. I just saw the sergeant today. Happy as a clam.

Some inmates cannot even address an envelope. There is a limit to my sympathy for a person in that case. It is inexcusable that you are 50 years old and cannot address an envelope. Needless to say, you need respect and have to look the other way with any comments to remain in your mind.

The first time I am in a dorm and prison, I am as quiet as a church mouse. I observe and observe and observe. You will very quickly ascertain who are the idiots and assholes (civil servants included). For that reason, I accepted nothing said by anyone as truthful until time passed and

I could acquire a sense of bearings as to what is really going on in a dorm.

This holds true in county jails, federal and state facilities. Keep under the radar and stay there until you have a comfort level. You may befriend someone only to find that person befriended you because everyone else cannot stand him nor trust him. He may be also be thinking that you are an easy mark.

Ladies...I use the masculine in this book for the most part. I have not forgotten you as much of the information holds true for you as well. In fact, much of the information holds true in any facility whether county, state or federal. Be on your toes, be on your guard and keep aware of your property and surroundings until you can "stand down" a little.

Many inmates suffer from serious drug problems which they continue in prison. They will sell their shoes and food for drugs or cigarettes. Both can be found anywhere even places where smoking is prohibited. Of course drugs are prohibited everywhere but it is around for a price. I do not understand it because there is no proper program to help people. ASAT, CASAT whatever you call it is bullshit. It needs to be fixed but as I never even tried an illegal drug (really!!!) I do not know how to fix it. More about that later.

The point I am making is you do not want to be associated with someone who is using a drug or drugs because now you are a target of the cops who will search you and write notes that maybe you are involved in something. No good. Stay away. It will follow you to every dorm, facility, cell and to Parole.

Many inmates suffer from ADHD. They walk around all day looking for something to do. They cannot focus properly and cannot occupy their time. Some program must be created to deal with this issue as I believe it does make a difference for if treated, it may in fact assist with a decrease in repeat offenders.

Some will draw, make cards, write poetry and there are some very talented individuals. I knew someone who had violated parole 5 times while I was at Groveland. A terrible drug habit and all the system kept doing was letting him go, violating him and sending him right back. I would joke that he should have left his belongings at the front door in a locker so he could pick them up when he came back. Sad but true my advice.. He has one arm. He makes ships, windmills, anything you can imagine and sells it for food. I can tell you he would make a good living in the street but the demon drug has killed that chance.

The most important thing you can do is understand that your fellow inmates have issues and you need to understand that and you need to respect that. If you do, you will be ok.

This One Needs to Stay In

There is no doubt in my mind that there are many inmates aka offenders aka criminals aka felons aka bad guys who should be locked in with the key thrown away. While I used to be a proponent of Capital Punishment, I am no longer for legal and constitutional reasons. Nevertheless there are some individuals who need to be kept away forever and ever. Inmates who have a life sentence are given a release date of 9999. While at Rikers Island I was in the North Infirmary Command or NIC for short. This is the prison medical center. It is divided into separate units with its own law library, commissary and recreation area. Religious Services were also held in a small gym area. The staff was polite, professional and not the bunch of rag tag civil servants as I encountered in the State System yet not as polished as the Federal workers.

Having been assigned to NIC shortly after I became ill was a concern but the benefits included visits every week from my wife who was treated with respect by the staff as opposed to the disrespectful manner in which the state civil servants treat their visitors. This was one of the reasons we decided on fewer visits upstate. The medical care was excellent and I was pleased with every aspect of the care except that once the doctor wrote "he needs surgery ASAP," the state snatched me up to do further harm to my illness and me. Big Brother Albany was watching.

Well... I met many inmates at Rikers. Some of which I felt sorry for especially the inner city youth who were being shot in the spine to paralyze them so as to avoid a murder rap for the shooter. These kids had colostomy bags, lost limbs and then there was the dry cleaner rapist. In my years, he was probably the worst individual I have met. He looked like the perfect neighbor, husband, father, son, professor, coworker but if there should be candidates for new methods of lethal injection formulas, please let him be patient number one.

It was not his first rape as he told me with joy and delight even though I told him on many occasions to stay away from me. He obviously was excited telling his story of attacking to women in the store and having them "do things to each other" as he pointed a gun at them and then joined in. He did not know it was all on camera. He could not believe that he did anything wrong and believed he was innocent and only helping them get over their sexual walls. He said they were excited by what happened.

I could not have been happier then when he was sentenced to 16 to life with a recommendation that he receive civil confinement.

While I find the whole civil confinement issue a separate issue which I am against for legal and constitutional issues (if you want them behind bars forever, sentence them to that punishment). In any event, he could not stop crying.

I hope he is still crying five years later in the really bad big house that you really do see on TV. I hope he never gets to experience a Groveland Resort and Spa vacation retreat.

By the way, not to generalize but I cannot help believing that sexual predators can never be treated. I have not met one who felt any inkling of remorse demonstrated to me or anyone else. There was a father at Groveland Resort and Spa who performed oral sex on his own daughter for several years and made light of it. There was another man who was found guilty of 192 counts (!!!) of sexual crimes against his foster children. He proclaimed his innocence every day. It was not his first rape as he told me with joy and delight even though I told him on many occasions to stay away from me. He obviously was excited telling his story of attacking to women in the store and having them "do things to each other" as he pointed a gun at them and then joined in. He did not know it was all on camera. He could not believe that he did anything wrong and believed he was innocent and only helping them get over their sexual walls. He said they were excited by what happened. I could not have been happier then when he was sentenced to 16 to life with a recommendation that he receive civil confinement. While I find the whole civil confinement issue a separate issue which I am against for legal and constitutional issues (if you want them behind bars forever, sentence them to that punishment). In any event, he could not stop crying. I hope he is still crying five years later in the really bad big house that you really do see on TV. I hope he never gets to experience a Groveland Resort and Spa vacation retreat.

The One Armed Talent

He lost his arm in an accident when he was a teenager . Italian, average build and now about 50 although he looked about 70. Polite, intelligent but full of the demons of Mr. Drugs and Mr. Booze. In and out of prison all his life his family lives in Florida and he had been fortunate to be one of the lucky ones-with such a long and terrible road behind him to loved still by them.

It is simply beautiful to see the objects he created over the years. 1500 era pirate ships about three feet long and 4 feet high. Ferris Wheels of equal dimensions. Using tools such as ice cream sticks, old shirts cut up and dental floss, he made absolutely majestic pieces which he has sold for hundreds of dollars. Even guards bought his creations. He could have his own business even on the streets of New York City or the beaches of Florida. The only problem of course is he cannot stay' out of jail.

During my four years, he had been released five times only to return on violations. The revolving door exists and the problem is that the State and our taxes are spent to keep the prison business thriving. I say this because in this man's case, he was medically unassigned because of all of his illnesses brought on over the years no doubt because of the demons. So all the State did in their infinite wisdom was to keep him locked up with no therapy nor treatment.

This is where the problem lies. Yes I agree that ones problems such as smoking, drinking, drugs can only be managed and stopped is if the individual really wants to stop his or her addiction. My friends case is the prime example of someone who truly does want to stop because when he is off the shit while in prison, he can accomplish beautiful things. I cannot believe with all of the research that is spent on programs this and programs that, there is no effective method of handling someone like my one armed friend who would love to get rid of the demons and be a productive member of the real world.

I do strongly believe that the system wants him back and forth in and out of prison to keep the business going. Another proof positive for my belief is that Florida agreed to accept his Parole under an Interstate Compact but New York has refused. Why? There is only one reason and I have already explained it above.

Guns

The world is tattooed. I have had the pleasure of visiting the South Pacific where tribal art is truly beautiful. To see the natural beauty of such artwork which is thousands of years old was very special and I am blessed to have had the opportunity to see it. Nowadays, it seems that everybody has a tattoo and while some are more attractive than others, many are quite simply just graffiti like writing and drawing. Don't think that only felons have tattoos. I have seen businessmen in the gym with a festoon of tattoos covered by their suits. I am still unsure what the message is. If the tattoos are designed to scare and intimidate or if they have some special meaning to the person. I think the truth lies somewhere in between.

I know members of the military will have them to honor fallen comrades and I certainly respect that.

I met a fellow inmate from NYC who looked like Sad Sack from the comic book of that name. Every part of his body had an issue and he was in a wheelchair, weighed about 90 pounds and wore a neck brace. Never showered because he was "allergic to the water." Baloney, he was just filthy. Never brushed his teeth with water. They were green.

But he had guns tattooed all over his arms which he would roll up the sleeves to proudly display. and rifles on his legs. Yes...he would roll up his pant legs too.

It was sad because no one took him seriously except to laugh at the tattoos. Other ridiculous ones were the guy with "family" tattooed across his neck. Could not figure that out. Others were done in prison and were complete messes. Others were done in prison and were beautiful.

To each his own. While this premise is acceptable, one can only accept someone else's personal habits and way of living until you have to smell it.

The Doctor Is In

Learning enhances my day as well as prevents a loss of or a vacuum of knowledge. I remember discussing Europe with someone who did not know that Italy was in Europe! Well...sometimes you feel like just crawling into bed to avoid more brain cells leaving your head!

Enter the Doctor. A mild mannered man who lived a very exciting life. Oh...by the way...not everyone who is educated is good in my book. The molesters still arriving to this day are pieces of shit whether or not they have a college or postgraduate degree.

The Doc studied medicine in Italy...in Italian no less. He was great. A motorcycle accident caused him severe injuries and a wheelchair.

His story was unique because I truly believe that he was duped by a drug pusher into having and causing his prescription pad to be misused even though I fault him for his misconduct.

He was sentenced to a 1 to 3 term. As a result, he lost his license and was placed in a federal database which denied him of course any access to federal insurance funding if he were to regain his license. The consequences in other words were far more serious than just the prison term.

Well unfortunately he was one naive man. He was constantly duped by the hawks and vultures who preyed on him. A few of us worked hard to keep them away and we were mostly successful. What was funny was he, read so slow he had a virtual hoarded junkyard of papers, food, and stuff (he would buy anything from anyone...clothes...food — etc.)

The real punishment was not against him however. It was his wife. His lawyer was not a criminal specialist and did not tell him that the 1 to 3 would really be a 2 year in prison term because he would probably be turned down for parole. He and his foreign born wife just could not understand his and now her plight. With no children and little if any family, she (who lost her job)n was stuck at home living a parallel sentence. While I do not think that the doctor deserved a lesser sentence (note to self: lawyer charged him legl fees in the tens of thousands and essentially ripped him off...he should be in prison), perhaps with technology today, he could get 1 year in prison and one year home confinement. Without the ability to prescribe medication, he would   be no risk and any intelligent investigator (if they exist) would ascertain that such bifurcated punishment would serve the public and be less costly that imprisonment, medical care and the now mental health treatment his wife needs.

There are other alternatives to incarceration but the State must keep the upstate economy above the water of depression by keeping the beds full. Stupid.

Pedophiles

I have written about these criminals in a few sections of this book because they do run the gamut of various areas of interest. None good.

While at Groveland, I learned that a majority of the population were pedophiles. Of course, almost everyone I have met consistently said they were innocent. Yes... I believe some are but I cannot believe what I read and learned about them. The man who performed oral sex on his daughter for several years until her mid teens.

The man who had sex with several of his step sisters and thought nothing wrong with it. The man who look at a picture of a actors daughter and said wow she is sexy. I ripped the weekly magazine from him. You cannot imagine the disgusting acts which they receive "therapy" for in what I call "sex school." Ridiculous. They are not cured. I am sorry but some sort of chemical castration or something needs to be done. I also find that the punishment is bullshit. For your first offense you generally receive 6 months in jail and then 5 or 10 years probation. Bullshit. If you file a forged instrument, you get more time.

Bullshit. Throw the key for at least 5 to 10 years and not at the Groveland Resort and Spa. How about they all go to prisons just for them and not at other places where other inmates must be with them. Also, it boggles my mind how many of them will be in wheelchairs, complain of all these maladies but as I say over and over again.. "the cock worked." Disgusting and bullshit.

These are the people that must be locked away. No remorse and sick, sick, sick. By the way, in prison if they are injured, it is a hate crime. You can get more time for that charge added to that which you are serving.

Chester the Molester

No insult to those named Chester but there are many in prison who are sexual predators who really know how to game the system. They will also try to game you.

One of the best examples is a middle aged man in a wheelchair for a variety of illnesses real and imagined. It always amazed me that the predators who were always innocent also had all sorts of medical issues. Some physical, some mental and some just all over the map. A common statement by me is that despite all of the problems, the c——k worked! Its true!!! Mr. B in my example looked like someone that if you saw him approaching your house, you would lock the doors, close the blinds and hide under the bed even if the kids were not at home! He looked the typical example of a molester. Well...he was and he used to "get" his victims by plying them with coloring books. Do you see where this is going? In prison he occupied his time coloring in children's coloring books!

The Program Committee never ceased to amaze me. Mr. F was an arsonist. They gave him a job as a welder! Sorry for the change of subjects here. Getting back to Mr. B he also knew how to game the religions. You are permitted, according to DOCCS regulations to change your religion once per year. Mr. B. knew how to do it more often. One day he would bless me, the next he was wearing a yarmulke

and the next he would be a Muslim. Of course there would be a few months in between but never a year. He was a Mormon, Jehovah's Witness and just about everything else you could imagine and still a predator. He too will be out one day.

Woodbourne

I have met many long term guests of corrections over the years. Many lifers and others who have just done decades in prison. The interesting thing is that it seems the longer you serve, the more relaxed, polite and mature you are. Perhaps it has something to do with resigning ones fate to remaining behind bars for years and years.

I had the pleasure to meet one gentleman who has been in prison for 30 years. He was educated having received his GED and College degrees while in prison. He was expected to be released soon. With his personality and his education, I am confident that he will obtain employment in a social services position and hopefully help those who need help. I must stress that I am in favor of education behind bars as Governor Andrew Cuomo has suggested. Governor George Pataki did away with the college program while he was in office. I think the money he believes he saved just went to bloating an otherwise already bloated state agency and state government.

Those I have met in prison who have their GED and even some credits towards a college degree tend to

be watchers of the idiots who come in and think they will play the Gene Wilder and Richard Pryor "stir crazy" characters "that's right, we bad." Society must recognize that most prisoners will be released and as I say over and over again, if we are going to "punish" then change all the names and just admit it: "NYS Prisons" not "corrections" we are just fooling ourselves and then let's further say we are a culture of "no."

Anyway, my former prisoner acquaintance would always compare Groveland to Woodbourne, another facility he was in for over 15 years. It became a home to him. The way we may discuss and compare towns and cities to others and the way we may compare hotels with others. It was sad and then I realized that it was all he had to compare to. Fortunately he has family, an education and hopefully as he has paid his debt to society and he will be a positive influence to others in his future.

Respect

Prison is a strange place as it concerns respect. Many inmates having grown up in poverty, lack of education, mental and drug related issues seem to in my opinion have very grandiose opinions of themselves. As a result, t h e slightest feeling of being disrespected can bring problems or as I call everything, "issues."

I have always been respectful to individuals so I commonly call people sir, ma'am, etc. For that reason, I find it was easy to address fellow inmates. I would suggest you do then same. It sets a good tone and results in the same respect for you. Likewise, I addresed the guards as officer and sir and those above a guard by their rank. It resulted also in the same due respect for you. Thank you goes a long way also. Little things matter as well. I never looked into someone's cube or room. That brings a lot of respect to you as well. Also if someone is engaged in a conversation, I avoided "Butting" into a conversation which is a no no. Even if , the issue is important, I leave it alone. I bit my tongue countless times.

Basically, the same common sense rules of courtesy and respect goes likewise in prison. The reason this is so much more important is it gets to what I said in the beginning of this chapter. Because of the various backgrounds of some people, showing respect is a given and it is very important that you show that respect.

Never cut a line and if someone does in front of you, caution abounds if you say something which I would not. You never know the person may be cutting in order to start a fight or distraction or commotion or just wants a fight in order to cut someone and or get out of the particular facility. It happens. Do not say anything. No need to be frightened by what I am saying but you should know some of these basics.

High Profile

Depending on your situation and whether you do federal, state or local prison time, you may find that you cross paths with various "high profile" inmates. I have met and seen and lived with celebrities, politicians, FBI and other police officers and officials, businessmen and members of several nefarious organizations.

Some of the above are assholes but most believe it or not are quiet and reserved. Most probably this is because they have been advised to maintain a very low profile lets they become a target for extortion or if too well known or high profile, subject to being confined to IPC (Involuntary Protective Custody). This status is no different from being in the "Hole" (Feds), "Box" (State), or "Bing" (NYC). There, your confined in a cell with little interaction with inmates and restrictions on phone, commissary and everything else.

Some are very proud of their notoriety and many will even show you newspaper articles and magazine articles about them. The level of narcissism and sociopathic disorder is, I believe, quite high. One individual in the State so loved himself that he kept framed photos which he changed almost daily and kept showing everyone his commissary and packages by leaving everything on top of his bed or locker. I also enjoyed him showing off when he would

get money and letters. No one cared for him. His sense of humor was ok but other than that, just another one who loved himself.

I asked him one day to show me pictures of his family as I would share mine and many other inmates would. He had none. This was because no one talked to him and only a friend kept him supplied with his needs. Too full of himself. Very annoying but I found him amusing. Others I have been more fond of because they were humble. They truly were remorseful. Others were plain scared shitless. It goes to show that if you break the law and "they" want to get you, no one is immune. Very interesting.

Inmates go through the "butt" cans in the yard and the leftover unsmoked tobacco and dry it out and resmoked it! Remember, anything and EVERYTHING for smokes. I think the state passively allows this for several reasons. First, it is huge moneymaker for the state. Second, it keeps the population docile because the smoking relieves the tension some of the addicts have. If they cannot have their drug of choice, then a "rollie" will do. A rollie is the cigarette made from a pouch of tobacco. If you can afford regular packs of cigarettes, then you are in possession of a brick. If you have ten bricks, you have a crate aka carton. I have

seen inmates do anything and EVERYTHING for them including literally selling the food off their tray in the mess hall. It is amazing. It is important to keep your personal property neat and locked in your locker. Thefts do occur. Remember you are amongst thieves. Most of the time they are discovered and , dealt with appropriately. I have been blessed to never have had that problem but you must guard everything as you would guard your house and car. Locked at all times. You also have a razor which must also be locked in your locker when not in use. Losing the razor is a 30 day trip to the box and $5.00 for the ticket.

I always had a lot of personal property but always neat and always secured. People would always offer me things to buy such as watches, radios, headphones, sneakers, sweatpants, underwear, T-shirts and the list goes on and on. Most of the merchandise is used but you will find amazing bargains.

Always negotiate in a respectful manner because the person selling may need pouches and stamps and to laugh is a no no in prison. Always show respect. Believe me it rewards you tenfold. Inmates always try to tweak what they own. A loose seam or some sort of creative wearing may show ingenuity. For example one guy wore his T-shirt sleeves up like the 50's because he had a tattoo of a gun. He was a little scrawny but it showed some thought process. Others will iron their shirts with creases running diagonally, vertically, horizontally or every which way! I could never do that but for a few stamps, they will do it for you.

Personal Property

The interesting dynamics of prison has worked its way
into the world of fashion also. Many who have do
not display. Many who have little display a lot. For
example, it is not uncommon to see an inmate have
numerous bars of soap and deodorant in his
cube/cell. This demonstrates that he is not only
clean but has the money to buy hygiene products
hence he has money. This holds true in both the
federal and state system. In the federal system where

packages are not allowed, everything is for sale in the commissary. As a result, there is little diversity because everyone is wearing the same color sweatpants, the same sneakers, radio and the list goes on. In the state system packages are allowed. Each facility can tweak the Directive 4911 which governs what is permissible. This lends itself to diversity and also an underground marketplace where you can buy all sorts of clothing from each other although technically not permissible. Normally, after the weekend visits are over, the dorm resembles a flea market with everything from deodorant to clothes to food available for a price. Again technically not allowed. The main reason for the flea market is cigarettes and stamps. Inmates love to gamble and inmates love to smoke. Not permitted in NYC facilities and not permitted in the federal system, smoking is a big moneymaker for NYS. They get their money from 'tickets' for enforcing no smoking rules in the dorms to selling tobacco in the commissary. Most of the time, inmates are too

poor to buy 'real" cigarettes, so they roll their own by buying pouches. The pouches then become the currency of choice. Inmates cot buy a pouch for about $3.20 or 12 stamps on the open market. Figure the math, it is profitable to buy the pouches and then sell them and use the profit to buy from the flea market without having to have your family send it into you. For example, you can buy a "alligator" shirt for about 4 pouches but if someone is "thirsty," you can get it for as low as 1 pouch!

If you smoke and have little income coming in from your family (the street as its called), then you will do anything and EVERYTHING to get pouches. I have seen some keep one pant leg up. Generally this can be construed to be a gang signal but many wear it regardless. Also colors may be used to designate gangs. This is one reason why you should be careful not to wear a color that is a known gang color lest you get caught up in a turf war. I wear them anyway but everyone knows me so it is ok. Just be on the "down low" until you get the lay of the land before you loosen up with your awareness level.

The package room in the state is quite an enjoyable experience. It is great to get called for a package. Some people do not get anything so I always shared my food, snacks and candies with my fellow felons. But remember, be cautious in

the beginning because if you arrive in a facility one day and then the next day start getting countless packages, you will also make countless "friends." That is no good. I have seen people lose their whole package to too many friends. A no no. I always got a lay of the land before I started to get packages. You learn pretty fast who you could trust and who you should be wary of. That said, sharing keeps a good atmosphere around you and when people get packages, they too will treat you. It also gives you some ideas of some other foods or clothes that you can ask your family for.

If you are in the federal system, you can only get packages of magazines or books. No newspapers are allowed in either the state or federal systems without a subscription direct from the publisher. It took me a long time to find out why. It seems some very intelligent characters figured out how to immerse a newspaper in some chemicals laced with illegal substances. The package room is also a great place to interact with the CO's. I say that in a variety of ways. Each package is X-rayed for contraband and must be specially wrapped in such manner so as to avoid any outside influence which means being opened and then drugs or weapons or cell phones added. It happens anyway but as time passes, more restrictions apply because of peoples' ingenuity. As for me, I am thankful to receive packages and as a result made a concerted effort with my family to send and thus obtain only approved items.

Hygiene

Hygiene is very important. I cannot stress how important it is to maintain proper hygiene. You cannot imagine the number of offenders who do not shower, do not wash their hands after using the restroom, have disgusting teeth if any at all and may have brought with them a host of diseases and illnesses. That said, I am sure that we encounter many individuals who are likewise disgusting with respect to hygiene in the real world.

I regularly (daily) would go to the gym in the street and also experienced witnessing many who would perspire after a workout only to put on a suit and walk out the door without taking a shower! The same in any office witnessing those, who do not wash their hands after using the toilet. While this is commonplace, it is seen more often than not in prison because you see the same people every day doing the same thing. This disregard may be due to the individuals upbringing and or dangerous lifestyle.

The excuses abound. Just this morning, the man doing the laundry said he takes a shower every other day because of a skin condition. Then... he should not be doing the laundry! He also says he does not kill the bugs

because they eat other bugs. This lack of concern for oneself and lack of respect for ones own body and that of others exist in prison and in life in the streets.

I would buy the double-ply toilet tissue in the commissary together with mouthwash and dental floss and toothpaste. Name brands are sold including underarm deodorant and antiperspirant. Buy it all and use it all. Do not lower your standards because some have less standards or none a$_t$ all. I should add that I also buy amino acids, Vitamins including daily multivitamins and vitamin C. I have also a supply of cough drops, turns, cough medicine and other products just in case. Fortunately that may have caused a protective ring around me because I rarely get sick besides my for preexisting condition.

I shower daily at home every morning, after the gym and each *evening before bed. I do the same in prison (except I cannot go to the gym because of my disability. I have witnessed some go weeks without a shower! No kidding, I will tell you that in max's, you are thrown into the shower with your clothes on if you try to do that. I would regularly make announcements that the water is free on weekends and sometimes would be nice and polite and assist some with hygiene products or offer to buy shampoo as an enticement to shower.

Other inmates are less polite and will force someone to shower

I would have my room cleaned with disinfectants which are supplied in addition to having the floor mopped and buffed. Everything would be wiped down. I never saw a bug in my room. I would also spray disinfectant around my windows and baseboards. l am a strong believer in keeping your area clean and doing or having someone do my laundry daily.

I must commend the system for having the public areas mopped and buffed several times daily as well as keeping the restroom and showers clean. There is no question that some areas and dorms are cleaner than others· but that is true anywhere. In any event, really keep after yourself.

The system also checks for TB and other illnesses regularly. That is important also and if you do want a test voluntarily, you just have to ask for it. You cannot waive a mandatory test such as TB which unfortunately does exist and if you attempt to waive it, you will be placed in isolation. This happens to be one of the few rules I absolutely support. you can be against this policy but it will do you no good. Do not do this. Some do it to "make a statement" They are crazy in my

mind but then again, they may well be. I also commend the system for providing gloves that we could use while cooking. You know that I will commend the system and powers that be when warranted and health and safety are areas deserving special mention and praise when they do the right thing. Believe it or not most prisons administered by the State and Federal systems are clean because the staff wants a clean environment also. The kitchens are also spotless. The kitchens are without question, maintained to high standards and each and every worker must be cleared by the medical department before working in the kitchen.

County and local jails are another story. Yes, dirt, filth, rats, mites, bugs, garbage abound. Fetid funk. A primary reason is that in local facilities, they are mostly transient whereas in federal and state facilities, people are staying for awhile and live in the facility for years and even decades so they have an incentive to keep their cell, cube, kitchen, laundry, shower and bathrooms as clean as possible. Painting, buffing, waxing and disinfecting a r e done daily. In fact, the some facilities are cleaner than many homes and businesses! Visit Penn Station in New York and have a look at the men's restroom and you will understand.

As for the fellow inmates, the story may be different. For reason that will never be understood by me, many people just don't shower or bathe properly or even wash their hands. Fellow inmates will do their best to bust the balls of people but do not be surprised if you see some inmates not showering. I do not understand it. I took a shower daily and sometimes twice and thrice depending on the weather and how I am feeling. The showers are safe in most places I was assigned. I went in, turned on the water and had what I referred to as the spa.

In fact, many of my fellow inmates began using the phrase as well as staff. All in all, it made for a tolerable stay. I made the best of it. The State has a subsidiary of the Corrections Department known as Corcraft which is an industry within the system that makes all the uniforms and desks, locker, soap, detergents etc. These industries are not unusual throughout the United States Correctional systems.

I used to think that the Long Island Railroad was a bastion of festering funk. People coughing, sneezing and all sorts of other bodily actions without covering their mouths etc. Well you are in for a treat because it is no different and at times worse.

In Federal prison smoking is no longer permitted. Same in New York City although the guards have been known to sneak in tobacco to calm the populous. In State custody however, smoking is allowed. I think a primary reason has to do with the money generated from tobacco sales. You would not believe that the vast majority of offenders smoke. Because of the high cost of tobacco, "TOPS" which is a loss tobacco is the most popular. It is cheap (about $3.19) and comes with rolling paper "rollies". Even this is too much money for some guys who have fines, restitution and/no source of income from home. They will sell their packages which their families send them and even themselves. No kidding. It is s shame and the state only does a rudimentary effort to stop the smoking by asking the inmate to put the smokers quit line on their phone sheet then call the line to get patches which many sell so that the nicotine can be leaked!

They will go without eating.

With all of the above in mind, the resultant smoking causes inmates to cough, choke and then spitting all day long. Included in this is the amount of inmates which use chewing tobacco and spit it out all day long. The guards are no better.

Gangs and Other Issues

First things first. Gangs are prevalent everywhere in the Correctional System not only in New York but in every State and no doubt in the federal system. Therefore, prison, a microcosm of the world, also has its share of gangs. You will be best served if you know that bloods, trips, MS13, Latin Kings and many others have a role in prison life. I have always been able to maintain "diplomatic relations" with people both inside and outside of prison so the issue of gangs is not an issue for me.

That said, you need to be aware of your surroundings and how you conduct yourself. This book is replete with information regarding that so I always address my fellow felons as "Sir", "Mr." etc and such formal respect goes a long way. Believe me when I tell you that I have earned a lot of respect. So much that different people would offer and have offered to "assist" me if I ever had a problem with someone. For the most part, if you keep out of trouble and the gossip you will be alright.

Most problems take place in the yard, weight areas and in the TV room. Your best bet would be to either steer clear of those areas or don't argue if someone changes a channel, tries to pick up a weight you are using or were going to use, etc. Steer clear of the groups of people who may be hanging out together. This does not mean

90

that you should not stand up for yourself if approached or threatened. If you do not, then you risk being subject to abuse for being too lenient or being a weakling.

It really boils down to being just as vigilant and aware of your surroundings as you would be in NYC or any large city. It is interesting how some who come from small towns can be seemingly unaware of these tidbits of advice because it can add up to you or them having an "issue" as I call it.

In NY, the State has closed many prisons of different security classifications. Primarily minimums and camps so there is now a mixing of inmates who have not only different crimes, different backgrounds, etc but also inmates with serious mental health issues and issues of violence.

I know a few inmates who came from the max's or "behind the wall" who could not adjust to the freedom of a medium. They begged to go back to a max and in some cases will do something to get their wish.

You will find racism across all segments. You will find skinheads, nazis, 5 percenters, etc and many have a deep hatred for others not their own. I too was able to make and maintain diplomatic relations but you have to see it to understand how they opine on and about others.

Do not be scared of tattoos. It is prevalent. Some have what look like graffiti on their bodies and it comes from all the different types and methods of doing it home based or in prison. Others have really beautiful works of art which are to be admired. I will also say that tattoos are so prevalent even see them in my hometown gym when guys who have them put on a suit and no one knows any better.

91

Bald heads are also in the popular category. You will see that in your hometown too so once again, prison is no different.

Always be aware of your surroundings. Always. Always Do not think for one minute that I am against alternate lifestyles. That is not the case. Having been raised in Manhattan and attending grammar, high school and college in Greenwich Village makes me sincerely a passionate defender of LGBT and however else an individual lives his or her life. What is interesting is that love does exist in prison. A lot of it. Many will say they actually hate "homos" as they call it only to learn later on that they were selling blow jobs for a pouch. No kidding. I was going to my room when I could not help but hear the moans and groans of a couple. They must have heard me rolling along in my chair because they peeked out, in full salute apologizing. This was mid afternoon. My comment..."I really don t care...go at it...don't let the wrong one catch you." That is my opinion. Sex goes on and on and despite all the rules against inmate with inmate, guard and inmate, civil servant and inmate, etc etc, it happens all the time. Again...Prison is a microcosm of the outside world.

I do feel sorry for those who have mixed feelings and believe that prison is a good place to out themselves because their family will not know. It can be a problem if you are caught because you can get additional time. Not worth it. I have always kept mine in my pants and there is no reason why someone with an alternate lifestyle would be so consumed with passion that they cannot wait to get home. This opinion does not apply to those serving super life and who are never going home. I can understand their situation. Also and most important...I have the most beautiful wife in the world and while I may be sailing the ss Groveland, for me...1 will take the spa and resort amenities and that is about all.

I do send my best to Frenchie, Diamond, Stephanie, Peachies and Boomer.

A Melting Pot

Corrections is a very interesting science. It involves many different personalities, psychologies, races, creeds, religions, and the list goes on and on. It used to be that no matter the crime, everyone lived "behind the wall" i.e. a penitentiary. Now, the system classifies inmates on varieties of criteria for which at the end of which, an inmate is assigned to a facility. This is why, at reception, do not think that any test they give you should be laughed at because it may be a factor in where you wind up. In NYS there are various levels of classifications based on crime, medical, mental health and other issues.

The State used to have, camps, minimum, medium and maximum facilities. The medium and maximums were then further defined as MedA and MedE and MaxA and MaxB. Now, for the most part all the State has are Mediums and Maximums. This has resulted in a noxious mixture of really bad and violent and psychologically disturbed individuals sharing facilities with meek, naive and otherwise good people except for the crime which may be minimal at best. Some schools of thought dictate that by doing so, the melting pot or blending of the inmates will serve to keep a facility more calm versus a place where everyone is a violent murderer. As I always say, no one forces you to work in a prison. While no one has forced me to do wrong, I am non violent and to put me in a facility with violent morons is a danger and cruel and inhuman punishment.

There is no excuse not to have the facilities better classified. If not, pay up when someone is hurt and cannot go home to their family without cut marks, stabs and other injuries.

Rules and Regulations

Every facility has its own internal, unwritten rules. You will get used to the individual rules and regulations of the different guards, sergeants, warden, etc. It is important for the most part to adhere& to them. Some are outright stupid because the rule was made by an essentially stupid civil servant. That said, obey them. The City, State and Feds publish their own set of rules which you must adhere to as well. They may be as simple as no smoking rules, mail service, count procedures and on and on and so forth and so on.

There are also Directives which you can get online to review. They govern each and every aspect of prison life including rules on how to complain about the rules. There is no sense in arguing about a rule unless it seriously impairs your personal health, welfare or safety Examples include what may or may not be allowed in the package you may receive and/or the type of sneaker allowed. I would suggest you just go along for the ride and work around it. You need to know what battles to choose and which ones you can simply laugh about..

I have come across some rules which are really stupid and without a rational basis. For example, you cannot cover your face with a hat while sleeping but you can use a towel?!?!?

No smoking in front of the building is another funny one because the guards do it all day long! Get the message and gist of it??'?

And The School Bus Goes Round and Round

Most prisons are large not only in capacity but also in acreage. The History of Groveland is very interesting. A Google Search will indicate that the "town square" was designed by the same man who designed New York City's Central Park. It is essentially a small town with a big fence around it. Old buildings and old street signs are a reminder that years ago, a community existed where nowadays a different community exists.

Security is paramount and a road circles the facility on the outside where a vehicle is driven by a shotgun wielding guard twenty-four hours a day, seven days per week and three-hundred sixty-five days per year. Think of all the gasoline being used when multiplied by all the correctional facilities throughout the country Because of the large compound area (or the resort area as I call it), two school buses (converted and now painted green) are on call for staff and guards to use when they shuttle around. One is driven by an inmate and the other (with tinted windows) by a guard. It is in one of

97

these converted buses that guard S drove (allegedly drunk) into the front fence and caused over 100, 000 dollars in damage according to my unsolicited conversation with an Inspector General.

Enter guard H. I cannot believe it is his real name because he lives up to it. He is tall, thin and has a

white goatee kind like a slim version of Uncle Sam. Indeed there are a few Uncle Sam and Colonel Sam's around. If you are dressed wrong, carrying something you should not be carrying, he will pull over and either question you or write a ticket. Fortunately he is sensible and gives you a chance but he always carries his rule books and directives and knows it in and out. found it funny that far his whole term of employment or a major part thereafter, he has spent all his in a little green school bus wasting gas and busting balls. I do not know but I find that type of job to be insulting and I would not want it. Perhaps it seems to be a job that while they say it is for security purposes (and in reality it probably is), it is a demeaning job driving around and around all day long and all night long for that matter.

Count Time

The most serious time of day is the regular routine of counting. Called "Count Time It seems that in the Feds, the guards will do it as a regular part of their job. In Rikers/NYC, it is also done as a matter of their job and security requirements but they don't care if you are walking around, talking, arguing, etc. They can count you in the shower, in the toilet, in your bed, in someone else's bed. As long as it adds up.

I should add that the Feds require you to stand for the count once or twice a day. The rest of the time you can be laying down and/or sleeping as long as you are generally quiet and in your bed or next to it. The main reasons for Count are to make sure you are alive (yes, we die in our sleep sometimes) and of course to make sure we did not decide to leave the comfort of our resort.

New York State is the best when it comes to Count. It is as if it is the high point of the day for some of the guards who have nothing else to do but sit and sleep. You must be very quiet and stand or sit near your bed as directed. On a serious note, they take it very seriously so do not even think of not being at bedside or not being quiet. You can get a ticket for disturbing or interfering with the institutional count. It is not a joke.

While most officers in NYS will count very quickly, some have to have another guard count with them. Sometimes because this is the rule, other times because as with Guard S, he is sleepy or intoxicated and needs help. It can be very funny to watch them do the count once, twice even three or more times because they got it wrong.

Routines

Prison can get boring but how you do your time depends on you. Keep in mind you are guilty, you did something bad and you are being punished for that which you have done. That said, there are things big and small you came do both physically and mentally. To a great extent, it is up to you to make your stay as manageable and as peaceful as possible.

I tried to maintain a schedule very similar to my real life. I wake in the morning about 5am and do some light stretching instead of in the real world going to the gym. My morning coffee, some note taking and diary writing and a few calls. Most important to my wife (I call her several times a day to make sure she is ok and the rest of the family. I call her (times approx) at 7:30am, 7pm and 9pm. Weekends about Noon, 4pm and 9pm. I call my mother also at approx

9:30am, 4pm and 9pm. Same on weekends. During the day, I will do my work and prepare for the next day, next week. I kept a calendar like I do in the real world. At night, I eat dinner (I am not a lunch person) I watch the news or a simulcast on the radio and then a spa experience. I call the shower my "spa" because I enjoy the hot water and steam and spray some oil scent (Muslim oil) and then stay for awhile. I now have everyone referring to the shower as the spa. Make the best of it.

Eat healthy. People snack all day and a few have worst diets and dietary skills and understanding. Not me. Coffee once or twice a day and then like Starbucks and Dunkin Donuts. I will "create" a flavored drink. Maybe a mochachino, maybe a cappuccino, an espresso. It can be done. I buy Fluff and that is my whipped cream! Be creative and it keeps you from being institutionalized.

Very important. You can either make the best of it or whine and be miserable all day. Either way, you have to do the time.

My dinner is also on plates and with utensils. Not spoons like many who have been in prison for decades and not in a bowl. I am not going to give the system a win by making me institutionalized.

During the summer which is a short season in Western New York, I spend time on the "beach". I know that sun worshipping is a very hot topic (no pun intended) but for me I am a sun worshipper. I stay outside as much as possible and my room has a large picture of a beach. In fact, it was painted a very pretty blue which I liked because it reminded me of the ocean. I spent about an hour or so in the sun every day the weather permitted.

The key is not to let the system win. If they do, you are finished and will never be the same. I look at it as a deep sleep or a blip and if you can maintain the same basic routine in prison, you will be ok.

This is the most troublesome aspect in my opinion of prison life. I am of the belief that if they put you in prison, they have to care for you. Courts will back me up because the system must not only keep you incarcerated (custody) but care for you. What this means in reality is subject to massive amounts of dispute.

Medical and Psychiatric Care

This topic is subject to a tremendous amount of litigation and definition. There are cases upon cases of prisoners suing for lack of care or negligence or malpractice.

The standards of care are different in prison than in the free world. In addition, employees are given qualified immunity which protects them in case of a law suit. Despite this, they have a duty of care and if they willfully _fail to provide such proper duty of care, they may be held liable. Keep in mind that you will encounter health care professionals who are excellent and dedicated and also those who are not. This is no different than that which you would encounter in the street.

My opinion and that which what I repeatedly uttered while incarcerated is that no one forces a Health Care Provider to work in a prison but once that person has made the decision to work in a

prison, then they are to maintain the, standard of care for which they are required to adhere to.

When you are first brought to a facility, you will undergo a routine battery of examinations including X-Rays, dental and general physical reviews. If you have any medical issues, it is incumbent upon you to mention and disclose this so a record is immediately made. I would also suggest that you maintain your own diary of when, where, what and how much on a daily, weekly and monthly basis or as is appropriate.

As the prison population is aging, many are getting medications, ambulatory devices and additional care such as CAT scans ₐₙd MRI's and the like. The cost to the system and as a result the taxpayer is tremendous and there is now finally a realization that many sick prisoners are better off home confined and at less cost to the taxpayers. If you have any records at home, have your family copy them and forward them to your facility for additional review. You have a right under Freedom of In laws (FOIA) to obtain copies of any and all of your medical records.

Psychiatric Records may be more cumbersome because of the sensitive nature of psychiatric records. Do not let anyone tell you that you cannot obtain these records. Keep in mind that you have to pay for them. Normally 25 to 75 cents per page. This is true in the street also. If you cannot afford these payments, ask your counselor because there are procedures to waive payment or to bill your account,

Most facilities have a sick call procedure. Normally in the early am around 6am. Sick call takes place not every day so make sure you know the days and times. If you sign up for sick call and miss it, you may get a ticket. In NYS a ticket costs $5.00. Avoid the ticket and get up. It is important to utilize sick call as needed to have a record made of your medical issue. Keep in mind that if your medical issue is later deemed not to have been an emergency, you may get a ticket. Some states charge a fee for sick call. The wait at sick call may be no different than in an emergency room in a city hospital. Be patient. I bring a book.

The system is sloppy, careless, nasty and uncaring generally except if you are really sick. If so, you must make certain to keep accurate, records and make sure your family is involved. They should call the facility if there is an issue. I was told once that my wife should not call because I should be my own advocate. My reply is that if you do your job properly, there is no need for my wife to call. Or, I also say that I cannot control my wife, who is a free,

taxpaying citizen, from calling. If you don't like it, tell her. They won't. In fact, your care will improve. As in our case, my wife was always polite and respectful and for that reason, her calls were far and few between but when made, received action.

As for psychiatric care, as I said before, prisons are the new mental health centers for the states. It is sad because there are some truly ill people who need help and as a result have no clue what is going on. Mental illness is of major concern. It is sad and sometimes you will encounter an inmate with serious mental health issues who really does want help but the system essentially has decided not to do so. It will take months to schedule a visit even in critical situations. I recall one individual who attempted suicide and was held overnight for observation and then released. Even when an individual meets with a mental health counselor, that individual will have a 30 minute appointment and then be scheduled for a follow up visit 4, 6 and perhaps 8 weeks later. This is not sufficient treatment and they know it. The outcome is that when released, these individuals will be our neighbors.

Cruise Ship Doctors

No one is forced to work in a prison let alone the nurses
and doctors. Most of them are hard working and
dedicated who for reasons unknown to me have decided
that they should work for the state. Maybe because of the
benefits. Maybe because of the limited immunity. Maybe
they cannot get a job elsewhere. By the way, I do not
mean to insult Cruise Ship doctors. Medicine and
shipboard care has come a long way and in one instance,
shipboard medical providers saved my father's life while
cruising The medical practitioners in the federal system at
the time of my incarceration were under the auspices of the
Centers for Disease Control and were part of the
military network in a manner I do not understand. It was
refreshing and reassuring to see them dressed in military
whites as the ones I met were in the navy. Very
professional and deserving of accolades. The medical
professionals in New York City Prisons were a step down
but polite and well meaning. Hats off to the doctor who
said I need surgery "ASAP."

Don't get sick in state prison. Only one provider who was a nurse practitioner is worthy of merit and praise as he did his job. I believe the job is several fold. First, provide medical care. Second, tell the bullshit artists from the ill who have legitimate medical issues. Third, be polite and human. Some providers have problems with this.

The judge sentenced me and handed the punishment. The state civil servants including medical providers had me in their care and custody. Exactly that.

There are cases and cases of negligence which only cost the state and we the taxpayers tons of money in lawsuits and assorted waste. Oh...by the way....on one medical trip I had the pleasure of witnessing a guard driving me stop in the prison parking lot and put a CASE of examination gloves in the trunk of HIS CAR.

One inmate was complaining for one year of a pain in one leg only to be "poo pooed." When he went home it was determined it was broken! Open the checkbook. One inmate was injected in the wrong ankle by a doctor with **medication which cost the** state a half-million dollars. One nurse was stealing drugs. Another nurse was bringing drugs in the prison to give it to her lover. She was a phlebotomist.

Even though I told them for four years my glucose level was high, they did not do anything for four years...open the checkbook in addition to the other pain and suffering, negligence, malpractice and the list goes on.

Why can inmates not smoke in front of buildings including the infirmary (I do not smoke). The nurse and guards had no problem smoking in front of the infirmary and all the other buildings and putting their cigarettes out on the brick walls and throwing the butts on the ground. maybe their butts don't stink???

If you went to see the doctor because of your heart, you could not ask him a question about your lungs.. You needed another appointment., This was to show "Albany aka ' Big Brother" that they were sooooo busy.

Waste. Waste. Waste. No excuse because even if you do not care about the inmates (and remember it can happen to you), it costs millions of dollars in waste and lawsuits because the staff could not care less nor give two shits about all the mistakes they made because Albany would protect them from personal liability.

They cannot get jobs elsewhere...not even on a cruise ship.

The Little Dipper

It is amazing that before I went to prison, l thought the most heinous of criminals were the murderers. Not true in my opinion. The murderers I met (and keep in mind that there are really bad murderers but they are in the maxes and the penitentiaries and I never encountered them) were of a mixed variety. Some were involved in drug deals gone bad but others could be you and me. One man walked into his daughters bedroom to find his brother-in-law molesting her. He shot him to death and was given 15 to life. Every time he went to the parole board, they hit him with two years because he was very frank and said he would do it again; Instead of giving him time, I would have given him a medal and proclamation. Not that we must take the law into our own hands but I am sure there are rational reactions which, while appearing irrational can be justified 'in the heat of passion.

The most heinous : the molesters. One of whom was a reed thin, tattoo laced piece of garbage who, while tattooing a young kid (yes a minor), stuck his thumb up the kids anus. Of course, like the other molesters I encountered he was innocent. A great conspiracy was responsible for his incarceration. Needless to say this went on and on. He complained of all sorts of medical issues including a back problem which, when being looked at while walking would cause him to dip thereby earning the name the dipper. Interesting that when he did not know people were looking at him, the dip disappeared!!!

111

Mr. Molester went home. Not even a few hours after he went home he was found looking into the kids window! Arrested and the subject of TV and Radio news coverage he was returned to the Groveland Resort and Spa only to once again profess not only innocence for his original crime but for the violation including the TV coverage!!! All a massive conspiracy.

RIP DAVE

Yes he was a molester although he said he was innocent. He had served about 21 years and had a few more to go. Wheelchair bound with a host of illnesses he became sick with the flu which permeated throughout the compound. Of course the guards blamed the inmates without thinking that the only way the illness could get into the prison was via the guards or staff.

Several days in a row Dave tried to have the infirmary help him with his flu which exacerbated his COPD and some other problems. They yelled at him for abusing emergency sick call.

I went to his cube to see how he was doing and he could barely keep his head up and looked as if he was ready to pass out and barely knew who I was. Around 10 am I told the guard on duty who is pretty decent and I could sense that he knew if he called medical, he would get an earful from them. He did call and did get the earful for "bothering" them. Anyway, Dave went down to medical and they had him sit there till at least Noon because that is when I saw him still in his wheelchair waiting for help.

Help came too late, he died.

If they are so unhappy with their work, go get a job in a real hospital. Maybe they feel as if they can just be neglectful and we will die so it is their way of dispensing justice. Either way it is wrong and terrible because it could happen to you. I would not want them to work in a hospital anyway with that attitude caring for a member of my family.

RIP Dave.

Jobs in Prison

Do not think you will be making big bucks. The average job pays about $2.50 per week. Then again, the prices in the commissary are reasonable but if you have a fine or surcharge the total amount you earn will be much less. You are paid on average every two weeks. A program committee will assign you a job based on the needs of the prison. It is not unusual for you to wind up in a job completely opposite from any experience you may have in life. This is because of the needs of the prison at the time and also plain stupidity on the part of those on the program committee. Also, they love the "big head' that comes with their very important position (sic). Often if an officer wants a particular inmate to have a particular job, the committee will do the opposite if they do not like the officer. Stupid but true.

Good jobs are hard to find. A wheelchair pusher commands almost top tier of about 17 dollars per two weeks. Everyone below age 65 must have a program.

The programs are called mods and there are four mods per day. You must have two mods. One can be an education or

trade mod and the other a job or double jobs or double mods depending on your personal situation. If you do not need an educational position then find out if you need a trade position or other vocation for time reductions such as Merit, etc, So be careful that what you are doing actually benefits you. There are clerk positions as well and these can actually be good if the supervisor is not an idiot or asshole. You can be a t e a c h e r s a i d e, m e s s h a l l c l e r k, d o r m c l e r k etc. If y o u h a v e a particular skill, try to speak to the person in charge of that department to get a job in that department.

My Ole Kentucky Home

There are some really decent people in prison- Many have had very bad lives and their lives have been made worse by terrible addictions to drugs and alcohol. It is sad to listen to grown men cry about their past. Homelessness, psychological problems, and the list goes on and on.

As a society, there is only so much the government can do but I strongly believe that our financial resources are so misplaced by a bloated system which cannot adequately handle the shear volume of those with mental and medical issues.

While I agree that our veterans deserve far better care at a faster pace than they presently receive, there is no excuse for a bloated government to ignore others and just throw them in prison.

Enter my friend JF who I met in 2011 when he was assigned to push me. I would joke and say he was "fried" and in a way it was true. He had psychological problems from day one of life including seizures. Perhaps an abusive upbringing and then drugs and old Mr. Booze. He would have good days and bad but we bounded despite both of us being stubborn.

He met a women who did him bad without a doubt. She had a criminal record and kind of leached on to him because think she saw some money in the family. Well here was the problem. JM is from

Kentucky and his down south accent was enjoyable to listen to although at times a little difficult to understand- He also had some short term memory issues and if I saw he was watching the weather on TV for example, I would ask him for the forecast. He would look up in the air, blow some air out of his mouth and tell me that "1 knew you were going to ask me." ..."Well...what is the weather forecast?   "I don't know!!!" I actually found him to be great for getting not only gossip, but correct information and details. I called him my cub reporter aka Jimmy Olsen and the head of the nonexistent Groveland Gazette. In all aspects of my contact with JM, he was and I hope still a decent man, respectful and dedicated and just dealt a wrong hand in life.

JM is an example of how the medical and psychiatric system fails. He would meet with a psychologist every month or so for about twenty minutes. No thought process in how unsuccessful that treatment schedule is. No doubt caused by volume and lack of money. I think if the benefits paid to some of these civil servants were reduced as time goes with the new hires, the system will slowly be able to provide quality mental health care with well paid and well benefitted civil servants. Otherwise the person in prison now will be your next door neighbor with no improvement in his care. The result is probably (and I am not speaking of JM here) a crime will take place, maybe an injury tothe public requiring medical care at cost) and then another one goes to jail. The system is broken. Please fix it.

As for JM, I pray that his life improves as well as his mental health and that he finds a women who will love him for who is and not that piece of garbage who tried to use his family.

Education/Programs

Work is a must unless you are over 65 years of age or are medically unassigned. Prison can be boring so take the opportunity to work. Finding work is not as simple as going ,to someone and asking for a job. Each facility has a program committee which will assign a job for you. The program committee is not comprised of rocket scientists. Someone who may need a GED may be placed on the waiting list and given a job as a porter. A 60 year old man without a GED will be put in school while the 18 year old!, who can really use a GED will be placed on a waiting list. I know someone who has a serious heart condition and uses or carries Nitro given a job driving a tractor! In the heat! Even the civilian supervisor could not believe it. That person was then transferred to a more sedentary job.

If you have a high school diploma or other school and educational certificates and college etc.; obtain copies before you "go in-" they can be sent by your family to the appropriate party when you are processed. Often they will not believe the copies are legitimate and will ask you to have them sent directly to the facility by the educational institution. That is ok but do it fast or you can be sitting in a GED class. It is a shame but they actually have classes for those who are essentially in a grammar school learning capacity. After they pass that battery of tests, they go to pre-GED then GED.

Sad but true.

Sometimes you are be able to go into a position you enjoy. Often, if they know you have some legal, medical or business degree, they make you a clerk for a department or you could be an assistant in school. Often, you will find you know more than the I worked in food service as the head clerk when I was in the feds. I saved them about $30,000 over a two year period and helped the assistant director become director after the director was transferred (i.e. promoted) after he saved $30,000 over a two year period! I loved working for them and worked hard because I respected them and they respected me. If you can find a good job, take it. It makes your time go faster. as for your truly, I was medically unassigned and received $2.25 a week. Some can make up to and over $20 per week if they have the right skills and work hard. As I said, it is not money, it is the ability to keep fresh and have the time pass quickly.

Because of my medical condition, I did very light stretching lest my body atrophy, walked a little and wrote my journals medical and legal, and also dealt with my medical issues.

Counselors/Counseling

Both the State and Federal systems have counselors whose primary objective is to push paper and meet with you every few months. The Federal system has a much better educated and qualified counselor system. As for the state, many have been been promoted and they have promoted within the ranks. For example, a former cashier in the commissary whose primary job is to place bar coded food products under a bar code reader became my counselor. One day while at a meeting with her, I used the word" exculpatory." I was admonished not to use big words that she could not spell nor understand. While there is a job for everyone, clearly she was not qualified for that job! They are supposed to tell you i f you need any programs but for the most part he system handles that automatically and you are responsible for ensuring that you obtain the appropriate programs based on your criminal conviction and work on obtaining them on your own by pushing your counselor. For example, if you are in prison because of a DWI charge, you will need ASAT (alcohol and substance abuse therapy) which is a course which essentially accomplishes nothing except waste taxpayer money and provide jobs. I do not mean to be cynical but unfortunately that is the truth.

The counselors (oh...excuse me in New York State they are Offender Rehabilitation Coordinators (I wonder if the cashier can figure how to spell that) also handle your approved telephone list. Another big, big job of nothing. In any event you will meet with them quarterly or twice a year depending on your sentence. Some of them are very good.

Most are polite but once again they are not rocket scientists. For those who laugh at my explanation of the system and think that an inmate should be lucky to have a counselor whether qualified or not, it is important to understand that as a taxpayer, that critic of me should know they are paying the counselors salary!

If you write to them (it is called dropping a tab) keep a copy for yourself. The state does not like you to keep copies because then they cannot try to say they never got your note or you never requested something. It is next to impossible to get carbon paper so buy copies at 10 cents each when you go to the commissary aandthen you can make copies in the law library. The copies are good as long as you are in the facility. Another tidbit..always keep copies of your commissary slips, receipts of deposits (monies sent in by family and others) and anything you receive from the state.

The Cashier

Counselors now have a new name. They are Offender Rehabilitation Coordinators. Big words for essentially a small job. Whoever makes up these titles deserves a medal for baloney because all these titles do is cause the civil servant to get a swollen head. I met only one Counselor who I believe truly worked hard for her charges. Ms. G made certain that an inmate's records were up to date and that all program requirements were met.

My first Counselor lasted until her retirement after 30 years in the system. She disclosed some personal problems at home which I sympathized with. Our professional relationship was cordial but limited because, the corrosive culture of no dictates that a solid wall of steel separates them from us. (Remember there is no such thing as corrections nor a desire to correct). Too much money is at stake.

I was told that because of my medical condition, I could not work nor do anything. She also told me that because of my education and especially my legal background, I was a "danger" to the corrections system. Translated to mean I know more than them and perhaps could not only help myself but others. She told

me that even if I "got better" I could not work in the law library. After two years at Groveland, I received a letter from her in corrections jargon...a "to-from." advising me that I was eligible for a transfer. I was excited because this meant I could move closer to home. I met with Ms. S and she advised me that she could assist in my transfer to Arthur Kill on Staten Island. That would have been wonderful but for the fact that Arthur Kill was shut down over six months prior to our meeting!

Basically all a counselor does or can't do is meet with you every three months to see if you are being sexually abused no kidding) and if you have any changes to your approved telephone list.

Then you are asked to sign a form. read it carefully and do as I did and obtain copies so that if down the road a program requirement is not met, you have proof of the issue. I also sent a thank you memo reciting what we discussed. (I did include the Arthur Kill story).

Ms. S. retired and I was assigned to Ms. S (not a clone but another s). We discussed absolutely nothing. She used to be the cashier in the commissary. While I am all in favor of upward mobility, this one took the prize. She asked me some questions and I used the word "exculpatory." She stopped what she was doing (which was taking a memo for the record) and said please do not use big words. (By the way, I know I told this story before. It is too funny to just mention once). Also, she said if I were to use the word, I would have to help her spell it. This is sad because there are many inmates who truly need assistance and to have someone who is essentially the only conduit not know much is sad, pathetic and most of all disgusting.

If the above is not enough, I still to this day have been unable to figure out what "Staff Training Day" is. It is every third Wednesday and all programs and services are cancelled. I really want to know what they do and I think as taxpayers they should tell us. Perhaps they can have a Spelling Bee.

Controlled Movements/Counts

Each facility has different rules and regulations regarding controlled movements and counts. Controlled movements means that you may or may not be permitted to go in and out of your dorm and/or cell unless the area is open for you do so. There may be movement every hour on the hour or so. If you do not adhere to the rules, you will be " out of bounds" and subject to a misbehavior report or as it is commonly known a ticket. Additionally, going to or from the mess hall may require doing so at certain times. Please make sure that you know the rules. Believe it or not it is very easy to accidentally get caught up in an Out Of Bounds situation by accident.

Counts are a part of everyday life. Counts are done either by you standing up or sitting at your bed or are even done while you are asleep. That too is a rule to make sure you are alive and that you did not put a dummy in your cube or bed. Many an inmate has died in bed either accidentally or accidentally on purpose and the count is for your protection as well. The counts can be quite funny because to put it mildly, some guards are not the best mathematicians. As a result, a count can be very fast or really slow as they try to figure out why they are a few inmates short.

It can also be quite pathetic as you watch the guards think someone is missing and then only to find them in their bed.

Some guards enjoy the authority of a count. Making sure its count time was a great source of satisfaction for one guard who I refer to as a real piece of shit who enjoyed yelling at the top of his lungs that it was count time then walked around slowly banging a flashlight He is a real embarrassment to the correctional system and should be ashamed at himself if not only for that but for being hands on, being drunk and for ramming a vehicle into the front gate causing over 100K in damage.

Let me emphasize that I support the purpose of the count because recently there was a spectacular escape making national and even international news. The convicts were evil individuals who needed to be behind bars but notice how the Guards were not the ones who eventually were responsible for the apprehension of one and the death of the other escapee.

Con Jobs and Cons

It is always important to remember that in prison there are criminals! Never forget that each and every person   you speak to has a history. Some good and some bad. There are very good people in prison who have done wrong and are paying the price for their wrongdoing.

There are others that are truly heinous and deserve to spend the rest of their lives locked away. For the most part, unless you are in a max where there are people "down" for decades and have decades more to go to get out if they do get out will you meet people from all walks of life. Remember as I have said and will continue to say, people are people and prison is a microcosm of the world. It is a small town.

Never give your locker number to anyone for any reason. The guards sometimes will remove an item or place art item in your locker. If you have given out your combo, you will never know what has transpired and blame the person who has the combo. This does not happen often but you nearer want to take the chance.

Never ask anyone to mail a letter for you. Do it yourself. You never want someone to have your addresses.

If the letter never reaches its destination, you will never know if the person you asked to send the

letter kept it. Also when you get your mail, remove the return address and tear it up. People have good eyesight in prison. It is called "clocking" and the pros clock everything at all times.

Always be aware your surroundings.

If you take medication, never ever sell it. The system, has excellent methods for tracking whether you have the meds on your person, blood tests to detect if you are taking it as prescribed and other methods.

Never ever have your family and friends on the outside make a call on behalf of someone. It goes like this: someone approaches and may or may not offer to pay you and puts on the sob story that the phone is cut off and asks your family to call someone to see if they are ok, etc. Never ever do it. An example of how this can go bad is if the person on the receiving end has an order of protection against the person in prison with you! You are now an accessory to a violation of an order of protection!!! I have seen it happen many times.

Normally your family and friends will establish a phone account with a company by depositing money into their system. You then tell your counselor to add that number to your list (15max) You can then call collect and the money is taken from the established account. The feds work similar and so too New York City. NYC allows you to do this online. The state is back in the 1800's. All they are missing are the two cups and a piece of string. But seriously, having friends and relatives making calls email or texts, etc on behalf of someone else is and can be very dangerous.

Never ever gamble. If you lose, you can lose big. It is a dangerous proposition.

Beware of extortion including friendly. Friendly extortion is when someone puts the old sob story of not having a commissary buy, no family, etc. You feel bad and before you know it, that person has literally become a member of your family and you are now feeding and clothing the person. I never allowed this and everyone can get a sense of how you operate. I have never been the victim of extortion nor attempted extortion. Maybe it is just because people respect me or other reasons not too mention.

I also had several "false" jars of coffee, peanut butter, jelly and mayo which are filled maybe 1/4 and my personal jars are separate. This way, when someone asks you to "borrow" some food, you can either show them how little you have or even say no. Saying no is ok. They will just move on to someone else. They are like bottom feeders

and are professional at it. I have seen someone for example "decide" to make a pasta meal. They have absolutely none of the ingredients, so they will ask one person for the pasta, one for the sauce, one for the cheese and so on. Bingo... a pasta meal. If you on the other hand ask them for something you will get the old bullshit "no" story.

Keep in mind there are some in prison who will truly have nothing and will give you the shirt off their back. There are some who are truly down on their luck. Those I help. They are very respectful and I cannot tell you how much I feel sorry for them and their plight. Those people I will do my utmost for but not the bloodsuckers and professional clackers. Absolutely no. In fact, if they ask for something I will let them know not to ask again. Understand that they know what they are doing so they will just move on to the next person.

Remember that cigarettes (pouches) and stamps are money in prison. A common scheme is to ask to borrow a stamp or pouch until they go to commissary. They repay you and then a few days later ask again. And again and again until they have upped it to a bunch of stamps. Bingo no repayment!!!

Also, some inmates have "stores" popcorn, coffee by the cup etc. Sometimes they charge 2 for 1. Beware of this because it is pricey and not worth it Do not even think of opening up your own store unless you are willing to "enforce non payment. That means trouble. Not worth it ever.

You may also hear stories about the Uniform Commercial Code (aka UCC) and how inmates can get tax relief, money upon release and that the governor is signing all sorts of laws reducing penalties etc. ALL BULLSHIT for the most part these are rumors that are years and years old. Be wary of getting involved in any of these schemes as the system takes this very seriously and you can get ticketed, boxed and perhaps for some unlucky moron get stuck with an outside charge. It does happen.

Regarding those who have little or are less fortunate,. I am very giving but also very careful that the stupid sign is not put on my back. For example, I gave someone a new jar of peanut butter. He sold it to buy cigs! Never again. Now, I will offer to make them a sandwich and if they think I am now a deli for a few feedings, then it stops. Then I can see who is really in need. Same is true for clothing. I have given away sweatshirts and thermals only to discover they are sold again. One even tried to sell me something i gave him!!! Never again for that.

Double Up

Inmates will spend their last penny on cigarettes-
Their addictions are so bad you can see an endless
cloud of smoke outside the dorms immediately
when the yard opens. At other times they will
smoke in the bathroom which is a no no.

If caught, you get a ticket. If not caught
the guard will close the dayroom/rec room for
24 hours. These guys do not care as the smoke is
more important than the food.

Because they have no money for food even though they
get three squares in the restaurant, they will resort to
literally begging. I do have a soft spot for those who
are truly down on their luck. The rest...NO. That is
the operative word and in fact, part of my sign
collection. A plain white piece of paper sign
that says...NO.

If someone is given food one day, they automatically
return over and over again for food, coffee, creamer, etc.
A simple yet effective solution is available. I have two
of each Peanut butter, Jelly, Creamer, Coffee and Mayo.
Very little of each food item is in the second jar. This
way, the person will see that you do not have much (and
don't worry, they do not care that they will use the last
amount of product contained in the "false jar.").

I kept the second jar only partially full. Perhaps two tablespoons of peanut butter, two scoops of coffee, etc. It really works. I am not an ogre and daily give all sorts of things but at my choosing to those I respect and respect back. It is interesting how word travels because no one ever bothers me but some inmates who will provide coffee and the like are swamped on a daily basis to the point they buy extra commissary to accommodate the requests. You will understand what I am saying here and this is very important because they will eat you out of house and home and you will be an easy mark. It only breeds trouble. There must be a limit to your kindness.

Some have many, some have none. As with everything else in prison, the divergent group of inmates also illustrates a divergent group of individuals and family ties. For some, the bonds are strong and for others the bonds are nonexistent. Many have a lot of baggage but that said, I do not know the whole story. I love hearing about all their bitches but they are probably people who just got tired of the abuse and lies of the prisoner.

I try to keep a low profile when it comes to my family. I am blessed to have loving family ties. A dear

mother, an intelligent and a successful daughter They have stood by me. And of course my Queen. It is very difficult for them to do the time with you. They do not and will not understand that which is going on every day in prison as they did not have this

134

book to read and can only go by what they see on TV and in the movies like OZ.

I have heard inmates tell their families they are starving and need a package. They get the page and then laugh it off and sell the food to gamble. I have seen a guy cry when his grandmother died only to learn he was crying because it was she who was sending him packages!

I also try to be quiet so as not to give the appearance of bragging because that will lead to jealousy and I never made to big a deal of my packages nor how many days till I go home. There are many never going home and I have also had some cry in my room because when they go home they have no home nor anyone to go home to. For that reason I am grateful and thank God and also know to be nice and appreciative to my loved ones.

It is also a time to find out who your friends are. I have a few friends and relatives who deserted my family and me and they were the ones who I helped tremendously in the street. They know who they are. I am thinking of naming names

because they should be ashamed of themselves for not even calling my mom to see how she is. If it were the other way and in some cases it was, I would and have called their family members.

Yosemite Sam

Western New York has lots of farms. I also learned whilst
in NY that pasta sauces, peanut butter and an
assortment of other food products are either
manufactured or bottled or canned in WNY. Still

keep in mind that WNY is a depressed and dreary place.

While Western new Yorkers may not like the downstate region, there are many differences between the two education, lifestyle and dress. I found all three while on vacation at Groveland. Many guards as well as my fellow felons would grow beards in the winter, shave their beards and heads in the summer and essentially dress different. Indeed many looked different, and acted different. A product of ones environment.

One guard exemplified the above. Guard G was pleasant with me but could be a terror to others. He was assigned (or in prison parlance had the "bid") for the Commissary. He ran it as if we were in the military and Yes... he looked like the Yosemite Sam cartoon character. A chain smoker, he wanted only 10 inmates at a time in the commissary (supermarket in my world!) waiting area a time he wanted everyone else waiting outside, in a straight line with no talking and no smoking (although he was a chain smoker as I have previously stated) in rain, sleet, snow, hail, locusts, etc.

He would get so angry his face would turn redder than it normally was. While I do not know if it was the result of drinking (a rumor of which I heard), he was very colorful to say the least.

He retired. I hope to an enjoyable post-prison life because he was respectful to me and only crazy with the knuckleheads. As for his legacy...none whatsoever. You can now talk in a crooked line, smoke and there can be more than 10 inmates at a time indoors, especially in foul weather.

New York City/Rikers

The two are intertwined. Think of NYC as a mini Fed/NYS except I would rather do my entire sentence in NYC/Rikers or Fed system than the backwardness of NYS and the desire to keep the beds full for economic reasons. That being said, I am confident that our present governor is aware of the abuses of the New York State Prison System and his doing his utmost to close prisons and address the problems which have befallen the state prison system. Kudos to him!

If you are arrested in NYC, you will spend the beginning of your time (which generally is credited to the sentence so keep track of the days) in one of the borough lockups. In Manhattan it is artfully known as the tombs. It is really not so bad because you have a cell and meals are brought to a central area in the "pod" where you eat.

After a few days if you do not make bail right away or after sentencing if you are awaiting your "state ready" status, you are sent to one of the many jails on Rikers Island. The Island is next to LaGuardia Airport so you hear the planes all day long. For me it kept me in reality.

The meals at Rikers are simple. Lots of jelly with bread, cereal and milk for breakfast, some slop for lunch and chicken twice a week. You can buy items in the Commissary with money your family sends in or can put into your account online. Really simple and not the archaic system the state has which has not learned about online payments yet. I believe that a primary reason for maintaining a paper only is to maintain jobs for those that have to process the mail. because the City and Feds have an online system leads me to believe it has nothing to do with security. You can use that money to pay for phone calls also.

You can get mail, newspapers, and magazines. Each person is given a "book" and "case number" which is quite long and which you need for everything.

There is a library in each jail, barber, visiting etc,.

Yes it is violent if you want it to be. Don't get involved in the bullshit- Also, rival gangs are around so wear nondescript clothing (you are allowed to wear your own clothing).

The guards are great because they are normal NYC folk with family and just want their pay and to go home.

If you look for trouble, you will find it. Do not look for trouble and it will not find you.

Holidays

Holidays are very stressful in the real
world and are no different in prison.
The stress is exacerbated by family
pressure and also by thinking too much.
It is better that you try to go with the
flow. Some inmates are really into the
holiday spirit and others are not. I wait for someone to
wish me a happy holiday before I do so unless
I am very familiar with the person.

Generally, the system will do its best
to "celebrate." For Memorial Day,
Independence Day and Labor day there are
barbecues and a special menu with hot dogs,
hamburgers and the side dishes. Sometimes the inmate
organizations will chip in and pay for ice cream or
during the winter holidays such as Christmas, Hanukkah
and Kwanza, donuts, cookies and cakes.
Christmas Day will find the mess hall
serving Roast Beef or Roast Beast as I
say!   Of   course
Thanksgiving brings Turkey and the smallest
amount of cranberry sauce the size of a
thumbnail!

I order from a great meat company in
Maine which ships boneless turkey
breast in dry ice. Same with ham, cold

cuts and cheeses. I buy a few different meats and Italian sausages and other guys chip in for some of the side dishes which makes for quite a delightful holiday treat. I make sure to buy extra so I can give those who do not have. Believe me it is appreciated. The ones who are jealous imbeciles with heinous crimes I will not give to. I do not make a big spectacle out of my sharing but I am blessed to have and share at home and share in prison.

Some of the inmates "expect" something. They get nothing. Fortunately, they are far and few between butI have no problem with giving to those who have little or nothing. They are truly grateful.

Wishing someone a happy holiday or happy thanksgiving etc is interesting and also a subject matter which requires you to walk on tiptoes. I have a friend who I respect very much. If you say Good Morning to him, his reply is "its morning." Reminds me of the old hound dog in my cartoon pasts.

If you wish him thanksgiving, he replies with good morning! Anyway, he will not eat on Thanksgiving Day. Only the day after! Strange but you must learn to respect others' situation even though they may seem strange to you. This is very imp**ortant.**

I have learned that some have had such terrible childhoods or lives or both that holidays bring back dreadful memories. Someone thanked me and hugged me saying that the recent Thanksgiving Day meal was his first real thanksgiving and he is 45 years old.

During the summer holiday season for Memorial Day, Independence Day and Labor Day, bands will play outside and it can be an enjoyable day. It is important to "play you're your mind." Don't torture yourself into being miserable because you think that is how you should be.

Too many do it and are of the mindset that because you are in prison you must act in a certain way. I do not buy into it nor should you. That is not to say I flaunt but I will interact with each individual the way they interact with me. Some inmates want to spend the day in bed sleeping the holiday away.

I respect that and let them be. Remember some inmates have serious mental issues and some have sad and terrible memories.

The system will also schedule services for the various religious holidays. I believe that they do a very good job doing so.

Keep in mind that for example, the Roman Catholic priest may not be available on Christmas Day so Christmas

Mass maybe a few days before or after. Needless to say they will have services.

Some people will try to change their religion to suit holidays. For example, there is one inmate who has beenMuslim, Roman Catholic, Protestant and Jewish in one year He gets the benefit of the special meals and services. I would always wish him the best albeit different ways each time I see him! He knows that I know. The system knows to but sometimes they look the other way. Normally, you DWI change your religion once a year and only after being interviewed by your "new religion." I think they use their judgment., My friend above is quite the character so I think they let him do it because they find it just as funny and amusing as I do!

I have always been religious and that always causes me reflection as to why I have done what I have done illegally yet pray every day for forgiveness, attend Mass weekly and have a deep spiritual belief. That said, the staff has gone out of their way to have a beautiful weekly service (Tuesdays at Groveland) with song and Communion. My hats off to a dedicated deacon and his wife who have been at Groveland for decades and to a priest who is a wonderful representative of the Church.

Keeping In Touch

Keeping in touch does not only mean communication with family and friends. It means knowing what is going on in the world. I maintained a regular line of communication via magazines, newspapers and the radio. I am not a television person so not watching TV in the common room was never a problem for me. It can be for some but TV can also be a problem. In some facilities, there is only one TV which is subject to the rules both formal and informal of the inmates and CO's. For my purposes it is not worth the hassle. I enjoy watching TV in a relatively quiet atmosphere. Not in NYS! The inmates who , scream and in general act like idiots. In the feds and in some state facilities, there are several TVs and you can tune to them on your radio. General quiet prevails.

Since I travel a lot, I enjoy listening to a variety of radio stations and shows. I found some of the best AM Morning talk shows upstate New York. Probably the best thing I have discovered in upstate New York. The shows are unscripted and not polished and gives you insight into how rural folks live. It is both funny and realizing at the same time. NPR and in general classic music stations are also lovely. I plan to stream these and avoid some of the NYC stations because I find them to be too polished.

A radio therefore is a must and each facility has its own rules and regulations regarding what kind. In the feds, you can buy an approved radio in the commissary. In the State, Directive 4911 applies so you must check that and the facility. In general, it must be clear and analog. No digital for the most part because some officers have complained an inmate can pick up their walkie talkies. Big deal, they have the volume so high you do not need your radio to listen! Also, nothing top secret is on their radios anyway. This is not the military. Their and full heads are too big of importance that does not exist. That said, you can also get an adapter to avoid buying batteries. You must follow the rules for adapters also.

I had a few cassettes (yes, the state has not allowed CD's in because inmates can break them and make ancient throwing darts!!!). Radios but find a good Sony for about $20 with one AA battery does the trick. I was even able to listen to NYC news on it and in the wee hours to Coast to Coast talking about UFOS! I also subscribed to the Wall Street Journal and USA today. They are inexpensive and because they are national, print locally and you can for the most part get the same day papers. Your local papers and even the NY Times can be very expensive

and you get them via mail which can take up to 10 days.

Magazines are an interesting story. Your library will contain a variety of relatively up to date publications but my wife would compile a group of about 10 magazines and send them to me via the package room. I would then exchange 10 magazines for the new ones. You are allowed up to 14 magazines and 25 books at any time in your room.

Some magazines are subject in fact as all are) to the Media Review Committee. I found this only with Maxim which have subscribed since its first issue over 10 years ago. It is funny and an enjoyable read. Anyway, I would monthly subscribe to Time, Maxim, Motor Trend, Popular Science and Popular Mechanics which would be delivered direct through regular daily mail call. The Media Review Committee would always find something in Maxim One month, they said the issue had article depicting martial arts. They sent me a memo asking what I wanted to do with the issue. I wrote and said to remove the "offensive" article and send me the rest of the issue. What did they do?

They removed a picture of a girl (fully clad I might add) and left in the article! Obviously the office of the Media Review Committee must be festooned with pictures of lovely ladies!

Keeping Up to Date also means preparing for release and I do not mean learning from Phase 3. I kept a folder known as "Post" and subdivided it into areas of interest from serious such as finances to the not so serious such as new websites or songs and movies I wanted to catch upon release. Any interesting articles about finances, and websites I would cut out and place in the repetitive section in order to remain focused and up to date upon release. This is important because a lot changes and fast in the world and this includes technology, clothing, cars and restaurants, food etc. I would read the Sunday papers and look at the CVS, Walgreens and coupon circulars including supermarkets. You must remain up to date so the transition (once again I do not mean Phase 3) will be easier on you.

Commissary/Packages

In the Federal Prison System, you are not permitted any packages. You can receive mail but newspaper and magazine subscriptions must be mailed directly to you and are subject to searched for contraband and drugs. All mail is searched.

In the New York State System, you are permitted to receive mail and also newspaper subscriptions provided that the newspaper is sent directly from the publisher. This is because it is possible to have newspaper "dipped" into some* sort of liquid chemical which can then be laced with drugs. Having no drug history or knowledge thereof, I do not know how this is done but that is the rule. I subscribed to USA Today and the Wall Street Journal. It is recommended because you will receive the papers the same day for the most part. Otherwise, other newspapers are mailed which means you may not receive them timely and thus may not receive them for up to two weeks later.

The prison library has an assortment of newspapers and magazine but my wife would send me about a dozen at a time which when I received them would pass them around to be read by my friends and then collect them because I had to exchange them in the State package room for new ones. Not so in the Feds and NYC. They did not care.

Magazine prices are really low and I took advantage of some great deals so 1 would have a few sent directly to me and this would save my wife some time and effort as well as cost of mailing. Since the Federal System does not allow packages, all clothing and electronics and food must be purchased in the facility commissary-Each facility has a different list of available products and perhaps more information is available online but this includes radios, batteries, sweatpants and underwear, undershirts, sneakers and all sorts of food from pasta to sauce, soup, bead, ice cream, beans coffee. I would guess about 100 different items are available. Each facility also has a 'buy 'schedule and that means you can shop weekly, biweekly etc.

The State system is different. A small assortment of clothes may be available but for the most part, food products are available. At present, you can buy $55 every two weeks on food products but keep in mind that each facility not only has a list of available items **but also what is considered** food. At Groveland for example, batteries are food! Go figure but if you understood Groveland, you would understand why this is so????

Cigarettes are not considered

It is amazing that you can buy more food buy more cigarettes and the like than food! The State wants their tax money.

Packages

The State has a Directive known as 4911. You can look it up online for the latest edition. The list is quite precise with detail and comprehensive and it is better to have the ability for a package of local home products that you can have bring good memories than only what is available in the commissary. Problem is that while I am grateful, each facility can then limit that list or interpret it differently. Before you buy, check with some people at your facility so you city learn the nuances of the particular facility before you are denied an item which must then be either donated, destroyed or sent home at your expense.

At Groveland, the Package room is managed by a CO nicknamed Good New Bad News. The name tells the tale. He would tell you that you have good news (i.e. a package) and the bad news (i.e. something or some things not permitted). They can be very picky but my strong suggestion is the nicer you are to the people in the package room, the nicer they are in letting certain items in.

Each day, your dorm lists packages that day and then you can go to get it. Never go down without being called or you are out of place. They will tell you when you have a package There are several companies which also deliver to facilities. For example (and you can check these online and maybe order a catalog) JL Marcus, Union Supply, Music by Mail and Bust the Move. I make no statement as to whether these companies are good or bad but they do supply a good assortment of clothing and food products. Again, Some facilities may not accept everything from the catalogs and you should make sure before you order. This is your responsibility. Yes the package room officer may be picky but generally this is because contraband was previously found in a particular item or a type of packaging which is easy to get into.

Certain colors are not permitted as are some sneakers because of possible "holes" or pockets which may be used to hide weapons and/or colors because of state regulations regarding prohibition of gang colors or symbols. It is your responsibility to check. Same is true with electronics, batteries, etc.

The Circle of Life

Not having ever used illegal drugs or prescription drugs illegally (yes...true!!!), I cannot relate to the devastating consequences of drug addiction. It destroys families and affects society as a whole in tremendous ways. While in prison, 1 have been able to not only observe but also interact with many inmates who know no other way of life except addiction.

We have also created a new class of criminals. Our soldiers. Our heroes returning from overseas defending our nation. When in battle, they are wounded and of course are provided with various forms of pain relief. Often, these relievers are addictive. They then use any means necessary to obtain their "fix" and in doing so break the law. While we say there are diversion programs to assist these addicts, often they wind up in prison. Filling beds and keeping the business growing.

I have also observed first hand those who have started their addictions at early ages uses pot and then gradually using other far more dangerous drugs. They go to prison. I don't care what you say, the ASAT programs don't work. I do not know what will work but I believe we need to seriously address the cost of these failed programs because while some of the inmates are in these programs they are using illegal drugs in prison despite the "urine" tests they undergo. They cannot shake the habit.

They are released to parole whether by the board or after their conditional release and then start using again only to return. Meanwhile these programs pay for and/or assist in housing, food stamps etc. Often they are too sick to work so they receive other forms of public assistance.

They then violate and once again back in prison to continue to   sad   circle   of   life.

Good Time

No, not the former TV program. In New York State, your sentence at the back end will have a percentage reduction which you receive if you successfully complete programs and do nothing to obtain "loss of good time. You can lose good time if you fail to complete a required program, refuse a required program, get a dirty urine, engage in violent behavior or such other act, action or omission which is listed as a possible loss of good time matter. If you do have that problem, you then go before the "Time Allowance Committee" made up of a lieutenant, a case worker and some other official generally the Deputy Superintendent for Program Services.a deputy superintendent.

It is basically a mini parole hearing where you essentially beg to have your good time restored.

I think this is excellent. We need them to eventually do away with parole as there are other alternatives as the feds have learned. This way the time is yours to lose and that keeps in tandem with judicial objectives and sentence plans. The Good Time process is similar to the feds and this way the penological objective of maintaining order in the correctional system is achieved and an inmate will receive a time benefit for that positive behavior and program accomplishment. It provides an incentive for the inmate to engage in positive behavior and learning which will benefit him or her upon release and also benefit society in the long term hopefully cutting down on recidivist behavior. Additionally, it does away with the Parole Board because it de-politicizes the system. Upon release, the parole officers are still monitoring the inmate for the remainder of the sentence thus keeping the parole officers employed and also maintaining a form of monitoring of the inmate for some time.

Stupid Stuff

As with any aspect of life, there are incidents, circumstances and events together with the totality of the circumstances which are funny, stupid and serious all perhaps at the same time.

For example, guards will frequently refer to State property as their own, i.e. "get off MY grass."

The following represents some elaboration of my findings:

Rumors exist in prison more so in my opinion than that which permeates society. You will hear about the governor signing legislation abolishing Parole, Cutting Sentences. I, without question am a Doubting Thomas in those circumstances and require written proof. Most of the time if not 99 percent of the time, no such proof exists . At other times, inmates will read a law as they want it to read. No Good for me and even though, as a lawyer I explain it to them, I can turn blue in the face attempting to explain why this or that is the way it is.

Guards will always be looking at their schedules because they are allowed to "swap" details. It shows that the state only wants bodies to fill the job and that there is no special qualification required for the job. That said, we need guards and to see

them constantly looking at their schedules and counting the time to retirement makes it strangely familiar to inmates counting the time until they go home.

Speaking of rumors, I once started a rumor that Jimmy Hoffa was buried under Home Plate in the facility ball field. Believe it or not the rumor started to swirl; What made it more funny was a few days after I started the rumor, coincidentally the ground crew needed to dig up a small space adjacent to the ballfield.The story took off!

Inmates will discuss the various jails they have been to as if they are discussing various jobs, travels, hotels, restaurants etc. It is funny and sad at the same time.

Remember to always shower with your underwear. There is a lot of homophobia especially in areas of the state where there exists less educated awareness and understanding of the various alternate lifestyles. Having been born and raised in Manhattan, I was exposed to various lifestyles so my awareness and understanding permitted me the fortune of being understanding and respectful.

Shaky Shaky No No

Compliments are a touchy subject in prison. Nowadays compliments can be a touchy subject in the real world too. Years ago you could tell a coworker of the opposite sex that he or she looked good. Today you will be the subject of a call to Human Resources and admonished for inappropriate conduct.

The same is true in the big house except the consequences can be more severe. Example: a fellow felon in my facility was incarcerated for a sex crime. I never knew the exact charge but of course he was "innocent." He had a very bad habit of telling one particular nurse that she looked good. While the comment may have been innocent enough, one never knows when it comes from a sex offender. Although they claim not to know our charges, there is no doubt that the powers that be know them.

About 2 am, a team of four officers with clubs entered the dorm silently and dragged this gentleman sex offender out never to be seen

again. More and likely he

was given a ticket for inappropriate comments and the charge would result in a "box" time which would subject him to being "drafted" out of the facility to either another medium prison or if the charge was sexual harassment then possible loss of good time and transfer to a maximum security prison.

Compliments are also a concern among fellow inmates. For example, suppose you compliment an inmate on his new polo shirt and then you learn that it is missing and presumed stolen. You are now suspect number one.

Suppose you compliment someone because he lost weight or otherwise looks good. Now you are branded a "homo."

By the way Shaky in my story above had some condition other than Parkinson's causing him to shake.

The Federal Bureau of Prisons controls the operation of the various Correctional Facilities in the United States.

There is no question that the system operates at a "higher" level aka more professional than the New York State system. The guards are professional. Many are former soldiers.

While the same may be true in NYS, there is a different atmosphere and in my opinion and based on my experience, a much better "experience."

Yes, the same bullshit occurs that 1 have described in this book vis a vis the interaction among inmates.

There is not the level of begging that goes on in the state and the guards are standoffish. You do not speak to them and they do not speak to you. The medical system is well managed.

The food is obtained through the military and the selection is much better. In general, there is a very noticeable difference between the two but keep in mind all of the generic rules and regulations are the same except, as I have said less bullshit. Notice I did not include the

New York City system in my description above. That is because, believe it or not, I would rather do my time in New York City custody than in the state. Without any insult intended, you do not have to put up with the hillbilly mentality in NYC or Federal custody. Both guards and inmates alike operate at a different level.

I was able to serve my Federal Sentence concurrent with my NYS sentence and I strongly suggest that you consult with your attorney so that he or she is able to work with both systems to insure that not only your sentences are concurrent but that the process is appropriately coordinated.

The federal system is more acutely aware of making sure that you serve your sentence close to home unlike NYS although keep in mind that if you are or

you become an asshole, they have the entire United States to schlep you around if you make them show you who is the boss. You will serve 85 percent of your time. No parole. Good. No need to beg fro freedom which after you do what you are supposed to do, they hit you anyway. If you are an asshole, you then lose the 15% good time. At least you know the story before the story begins. Remember, it is still prison and the "supervised release" for the 15% will be managed by officials who will treat you as you treat them. Don't play around and all will be well. I was fortunate to "self surrender." a few days before your date of incarceration begins (after your sentencing), you will receive details as to where and when you are to report. It is imperative you show up otherwise the United States Marshal will find you and now your sentence will suffer. Do not be an idiot with the privilege of self surrender afforded you.

163

The BOP operates clusters of facilities known as Federal Correctional Complexes of which there is contained within a Penitentiary, A Medium, a Low and a Camp. Depending on your sentence and time and security classification you will be assigned and/or transferred as the case may be to the various complexes and facilities contained therein. There are also "local" holding areas in metropolitan areas known as Metropolitan Detention Centers. Kind of a county jail so to speak which will then be your home until you make bail or eventually are sentenced and then transferred to a facility. They also have, for the real "bad" people, facilities in Marion and in Colorado known as ADX (or Administrative Detention Center - Maximum. They are essentially Super Maximum Security Facilities. This is where the bad boys really are and the guards to match.

Guards in general wear uniforms but are spick and span polished with a blazer, clip on tie and shiny shoes with crisp shirts and pants. DO not bother them and they will not bother you.

The facilities are generally better than state facilities. You cannot get any packages whatsoever but the commissary contains everything from food to clothing and electronics. You use the money you earn while working plus any money sent in from the outside. There are phones with restrictions and email with similar restrictions which you must adhere. The feds are doing their best to limit their population but keep in mind if your crime is bad, you will do time. Time by the way is measured in months. 30 years is 360 months. 1 do not know which sounds better but 30 years or 360 months is a long time.

The facilities are in general very clean. There are multiple TV's in some facilities so there is no arguments over what to watch. beneath each TV is a corresponding station which you can listen to on your own personal radio. The TV room is quiet. There are microwaves and also card rooms where the noise level is a little higher.

Prison is still prison but New York has a lot to learn especially the politically saturated parole system and obese bureaucracy designed to keep the beds full so the upstate economy at least resembles a civilized society.

I do commend the Governor for closing prisons and understanding that there exists a bloated

infrastructure which he is at least addressing.

The Mattress

Once you get the lay of the land and begin to know your fellow inmates, it is easy to tell the good from the bad. Yes, just because we are felons does not mean that everyone is bad just like not all cops are good.

For the above reason, you tend to rely on each other to watch over you. Not in a protection kind of way but in other ways like wake you up for count, remind you that the water is boiling in the microwave, make a cup of coffee, etc. Enter the Mattress.

While in Allenwood, I was in the company of some "businessmen." One in particular was going to be resentenced at the Federal Court in Valhalla. The procedure is you are packed up so your belongings are not stolen and you are then shipped off to where you are supposed to be several weeks in advance. You then return to your "home" facility after conclusion of your matter. So one

day, my friend D approaches me and asks if I can watch over something for him while he is gone. Of course I reply only happy to help out. Re shows me his mattress! It was a custom made mattress the kind of which you would want in your home. I asked no questions like where or how did you get it. In any event he said he would be gone about 6 weeks. Tell, the round trip turned into 6 months and I felt as if I were a bird waiting for the egg to hatch but for 6 months I had the most comfortable mattress in the entire correctional system! When he returned, he could not be more pleased and grateful that the mattress was clean and intact.

Several years later I happened to meet one of his friends in the street and it was funny because as we chatted, he said to me, "hey, you watched D's mattress!"

Gotta Make the Sauce

A highlight of the week is the ability to cook_ I always enjoyed cooking as I find it relaxing and a time to create, and especially to make other people happy. I love to see my daughter, wife and family enjoy my cooking and on holidays, have the family over for all the fixings. They keep coming back so it must mean I am doing something right for a change!

Same in prison. I cook once a week or so because the , rest of week I will eat a sandwich, PB & J or something real simple. I may also contribute so that someone else cooks and I buy in. When I cook, I make sure l have all the ingredients. If am going to do it , I will do it rights or not at all.

In Allenwood (feds) I would eat with a few guys and every Sunday we would eat in a small side room we could reserve. Enter the Sauce. Every week someone else would make the sauce. Keep in mind we do not have proper utensils so improvs are necessary. The sauce bowl is the foot bowl you get in medical. Glean of course! Same in the State although we were able to get larger bowls through the package room. Some facilities do not allow large bowls so check with your facility as they may be grandfathered like Groveland.

Well, it was my turn and since I was eating with some guys you may have read about in the newspapers or have seen on TV, I was nervous.

I am not the nervous type nor one to be intimidated easily but I was nervous.

The commissary sold POMS sauce which I added garlic, onions and some other tidbits and guess what....They like it! I passed the test. Same in State prison. No one has gotten sick from my cooking even if I cooked in a foot bowl!

Federal Prisoner Coming Through

After 18 months at Allenwood (Federal Prisoners are sentenced in months...360 months is not so good), I was ready to leave, go to NYC jail and then be transferred to State custody for the trip "upstate."

The logistics of transferring a prisoner are quite complicated because it is based on your security level which mine was always low and whether you are violent (in Rikers, violent inmates wear little mittens when being transported) and other factors such as mental stability, risk of flight, etc.

The protocol called for me to be transferred by US Marshal's to the local county jail until NYC could pick me up and transport me to Rikers to await the transfer upstate.

I was shackled lick Hannibal Lechter (imagine if I had a high security level) and then put into an unmarked van with US Marshals. When I arrived at the County Jail a few people were on the sidewalk and in the area leading into the building. Wielding big weapons, one of the Marshall's yelled "federal prisoner coming through." Loud enough that everyone turned including me because for a moment I did not know they meant me!!!

I was the placed in a dark damp cell something out of an old western movie. It took about four days for NYC to pick me up but in the interim I was stuck in a real jail like you see on TV. As I entered the cell with only a bare light bulb in the ceiling and a bunk bed, I heard a whimper. I turned to see a young kid lying on the bed crying. He kept saying "I cannot take it." Being the kind old sort I am, I asked him if he were ok.

"I can't take it."

"It will be all right. How much time do you have."

"Thirty days"

You motherfu---r, you open your mouth one more time and ....!"

He was quiet for the rest of my time in Mayberry.

174

Reform?

This is a very difficult subject. Many die-hard liberals and die-hard conservatives will have firmly rooted beliefs. These beliefs are based on socioeconomic upbringing, education, lifestyle, and other demographics which may or may not have to do with having any experience whatsoever with the criminal-justice system. Everyone must understand that Big-Brother is out there. While there are benefits to this, we must also understand that the drawbacks can have severe consequences.

Advances in metadata capture, facial recognition, license plate scanners and other methods of tracking are not only being used to prevent terrorism but also in every day life. 1 remember when EZPass was established. The information was supposed to be kept private as was cell phone calls and text messaging. Now, today, the information may be obtained by parties in divorce actions to see if the other spouse was engaged in carnal coupling. Soon, facial recognition will be used to show a spouse leaving a jewelry store and software data will show what he or she bought and cameras will capture the individual going to/from the hot sheet hotel.

Laugh about this but before you know it, each and every movement will be used in tax actions (why did you have a steak in three different restaurants over the course of one week and you told us (the IRS) that you cannot pay your tax bill)?

While these tools may have marketing advantages also, they also may have repercussions in the criminal justice system. After the camera catches you wobbling out of a bar, the credit card you used to pay for your bill alerts your automobile insurance company that you had three drinks in 30 minutes. Start your car. A device is alerted and your license plate is entered into a system so the police can be made aware of your tipsiness. Having the ability to scan hundreds of plates per minute, you are pulled over. Arrested. With the evidence against you, your lawyer advises you to plead guilty. Perhaps the Assistant District Attorney wants another plea this week or else his or her boss will be opposed to a raise or promotion. You plead guilty in exchange for 1 to 3 years in prison. You accept the offer not realizing that the 1 to 3 year term is really 2 years in prison.

An interesting aspect of being in prison is the punishment inflicted by the government and its impact down the line with respect to Social services. When you are in prison, you are not entitled to continue to receive Social Security if in fact you were a recipient prior to your incarceration. This includes SSI, SSD and retirement Social Security.

While this makes sense on a surface level, the impact is not only interesting but deserves rethinking.

I know of many people who, yes the y are guilty and deserve punishment but their families are still on the outside.

The reduction in the entitlement as it is lawfully called results in the family now receiving less income therefore unable to pay for rent, mortgage etc. They now go on welfare, receive food stamps, Medicaid, etc. They may lose their homes or become delinquent in rent and upon release may have to go to a homeless shelter. Therefore while the underlying concept of punishing the inmate with the stoppage of the benefit, the government winds up paying more in the long run because the government now has to pay for the consequences of the stoppage in additional benefits and support including health insurance for the family and eventually the incarcerated when he or she is released and the entitlement starts again the damage has been done.

The desire to keep the beds full is evident in a Wall Street Journal Article about a NY State Assistant Attorney General who wrote a letter (positive to the Parole Board about an inmate and was fired. These cases go on and basically prove what everyone really knows is that keeping the beds full is great for the Upstate/Western New York economies because the reality is there is nothing else up in those parts except prisons.

The feds are doing their best to reduce the population with a review of the sentencing structure. New York would be wise to do so also. Abolish Parole and the ridiculous corruption and waste of taxpayer money and follow the feds and other states with an 85% sentencing structure. It can be done.

Recently, I noticed that inmates are being selected to sign up for Medicaid. I knew there had to be some financial bullshit behind this apparent "wonderful deed" by the State and I found it Mow, if an inmate goes to an outside hospital, who pays? Medicaid. This way, the budget expense shifts out of DOCCS so there is still the incentive to keep the beds full but the overall budget can be argued by DOCCS as not being so excessive because some medical expenses need not be reported because they are being paid by Medicaid. Still, the taxpayer pays. Do not be fooled, this is a Ding game and the people who think up these schemes should themselves be behind bars for flee icing the taxpayers to quote a former US Senator William Proxmire.

All In The Family

Unlike the Federal system. Prison System, nepotism is rampant in New York State. For example, a sergeant is married to a nurse. A captain is related to an Inmate Accounts worker. The daughter of the superintendent (warden as I like to say) is a nurse.   There are also husband and wives married who work in the same facility . Essentially, the system fosters this type of nepotism. Oh...there are also a few sons and fathers as there are also fathers and daughters.

My problem with this is that not only does it cause a systemic dysfunction where you have generations of people working for the state instead of perhaps obtaining higher education, you have a bunch of civil servants being supported by the taxpayers.

Where it becomes dangerous is if one of the individuals has an issue with a fellow worker or inmate. When that happens you have fights, beatings and the associated problems thereof which are now enhanced. My suggestion is that if there is a relation (and I am certain that many of these relationships are hidden and not disclosed) then the parties involved do not work at the same prison.

There was an ongoing love fest between an officer and another officer who kind of looked like Fred Flintstone. While I am certain Fred never beat up Wilma, the same could not be said of this piece of shit which did beat up his "beloved." He would walk around the dorm picking up an extra blanket, cup, whatever an inmate had which did nothing to disturb security and do it when the inmate was not around. A sneak thief as it is called. He was such a piece of shit that some officers would not let him in their dorms when he was on duty! Anyway, one day they found him dead as a doorknob in an officers room. The moral. of the story is that shit is shit shit is shit whether you are wearing blue or green. Another moral of the story is to stop the nepotism as T have witnessed firsthand the problems it causes.

I wonder what would happen to the socioeconomic structure of Western New York without the nepotism and the prison system. Please do not misunderstand me. We need prisons because there are really bad people who need to be away from society (and little kids). But we do not need prisons to maintain an economy.

It could happen to you.

The State has Bunches of Money

I marvel at the waste I witnessed and can only write about some of it although the list can go on and on. This section is not about the judicial waste of the system but little items here and there that together I am certain adds up.

A few days after New Years 2015 each and every cube was given a brand new laundry bag with the cube name and number assigned. Let's say 50000 for the entire state. A pretty pretty.

New Windows are being installed, heavy duty with bars requiring a fork lift. These windows are for buildings without inmates sleeping in them! Basically school and offices. Makes no sense.

Why can't we take toast out of the mess hall in the morning but can take 4 slices of bread out for lunch and dinner meals? Don't think that it is because toast is prohibited in the dorms. Each dorm has a toaster! Oh...they count the slices!

Why can't we take fruit out of the mess hall? Don't think it is because we cup, make "hooch." We can get unlimited amounts of fruit through the package room up to a total package of 35 pounds!

Why are all the lights burning during the day. Shut off half. Don't say it is for security purposes because they are off on weekends   and   during   the   evening.

The entire system from federal, state and local is fraught with corruption, bureaucracy, bloated management. It is a massive business with solutions in sight but who knows when the solutions will actually result in a system that can fairly meet out justice.